Parenting: The Best Joy I've Ever Had

LaSonya Young

Editor: Sharp Editorial

Disclaimer: This book is not meant to diagnose or heal. This book is for informational purposes only. Everything in this book may not work for you. If you find something that works, even if it is only one thing, work it and make it your own. I pray you to find this information useful.

joy

[joi]

NOUN

a feeling of great pleasure and happiness.

synonyms: delight. joyfulness. jubilation. triumph. exultation.

rejoicing.

Dedication

First, thank You, Jesus! You are magnificent, wonderful, and full of sweet grace!

To my husband: Rick. Thank you for your persistent dedication to our family. I love you!

To my children: Jennifer, Brittany, Josh, Amber, Bridgette, and Aaron. Thank you for being so amazing and letting us practice with you. Thank God we made it!

To my sweet grandbabies: Max, Tre, Zuri, Anaya, Ruby, Zaina, and Noa, my future grands, great-grands, and many generations to come. There are no words to express my love for you. Just know I love you to the moon and beyond!

Acknowledgments

I have the most amazing mother, Elzora Massey.

Mom, when I was a teenager, I wanted to grow up and be just like you. I wanted to be the type of mother that you are to my siblings and me. As a single mother of eight, you did everything to see that we traveled, were educated, and never went a day without feeling loved. You made sure I knew I came from a line of strong Black women. As a child, you played with me, ran races with me, disciplined me, and always came to my rescue. One of my favorite times in life was when we traveled Europe together. Mom, you are still the most amazing example of motherhood. You are simply the best, my dear! I only hope that I am half the mother to my children that you are to me. Remember, we will always have Paris!

Table of Contents

Aforethought

A society must be judged by how it treats its most vulnerable —and most valuable members: its children. The State of America's Children 2020 makes it abundantly clear that by this measure, America is falling shamefully short.
Children's Defense Fund

Nearly 700,000 children are abused in the U.S each year. Child welfare authorities ensure the safety of more than 3.5 million kids.
National Children's Alliance

"It is in the homes and in childhood that the wreckage of human life begins."
Katharine Tingley

A Note to the Reader

"The elimination diet: Remove anger, regret, resentment, guilt, blame, and worry. Then, watch your health and life improve."

Charles F. Glassman

How do or did you feel about having a baby?

Were you excited?

Nervous?

Devastated or resentful?

If you feel the latter, it is important to deal with these feelings. The last thing you should want is to unintentionally pass unresolved feelings on to your child(ren); that could be the start of other problems to last a lifetime for you and them. You must become aware of your unresolved issues and seek to resolve them.

Of course, parents have fears regarding having their first child or additional children. When speaking with parents, I hear the same fears about the delivery process, the baby's health, and providing for their children. According to *New*

York Post, parents worry most about their child's overall well-being, specifically their child's physical health (95 percent) (Gervis 2018). Those are normal fears, but there may be a problem when fear becomes consuming and maladaptive. If you experience persisting fears that constantly affect your sleep and eating habits, have thoughts of self-harm or hurting others, extreme depression, or anxiety about being a mom, or are not coming to grips with the thought of being a mother, please do not take those feeling lightly. It is time to seek professional help, such as a local counselor, community health center, or virtual counseling. The old saying "hurt people hurt people" is true, and often, the people we hurt are our children.

According to the National Children's Alliance, 78% of children were victimized by a parent in substantiated child abuse cases ("National Child Abuse Statistics from NCA" 2021).

Seventy-eight percent of abused children are abused by a parent?

That statistic is frightening and breaks my heart, yet many people turn a blind eye to this truth. People are in crisis mode in their homes, yet very few people are talking about it.

The American Society for the Positive Care of Children (SPCC) reports that "five children die every day from child abuse" (American SPCC 2014). In some cases, the abuser may not have intended to cross the line, but they did. Therefore, it is so important to seek help.

Think about how many people in this world are parents and how many have been parents; the number is staggering, yet not one person has been a perfect parent. None of us are without flaws. Being a perfect parent does not exist! Perfection is unrealistic. So, if perfection is what you are hoping for, accept that it won't happen. However, you can be present, loving, and kind. Exercise simple kindness from one human to another. The other human just happens to be your child. Just remember that the love you have for yourself will pass on to your child. Every child deserves to be loved and feel safe.

Introduction

"Once your mindset changes, everything on the outside will change along with it."

Steve Maraboli

When I was blessed with my first child, a little girl, I was smitten. There she was, pretty in pink, soft as cotton, strong as molasses, and sweet as a baby could be. As I held her in my arms and touched her beautiful brown face, I thought to myself, "What can be compared to the softness of her skin?" Her sweet baby breath was like a praise song about all that was right in the world, and I had been blessed to sing along.

As her little eyes gazed upon me, they paralyzed me. I held my breath. I couldn't move. I knew she saw something, perhaps an angel, and I did not want to disrupt what God was allowing her to see. Her tiny hands and feet fit just inside my hand. As I held them, I felt as if I handled pure gold, nothing less. She was my gift from God. This little one that had filled my tummy, dreams, and heart now filled my world, and oh, what a wonderful world!

This may be hard to believe, but I experienced this joyous feeling with all six of my children. God must love me so much to give me such precious ones. In return, through this book, I want to help moms find the joy of being a mommy. I want to share parenting tips, things I got right, mistakes I made, lessons learned, and notes to self I made along the way. The one constant amid this parenting journey is that parenting will always be one of my greatest joys. I'm sharing my joy and love for parenting in hopes of promoting a shift in your mindset when dealing with children, transitioning from job to joy, burdensome to joy, and feeling overwhelmed to experiencing joy.

There are many negative voices and attitudes about raising children. Just because others do not enjoy the parenting experience does not mean that you can't or shouldn't. Do not let others determine how you feel about being a parent. People with bad marriages may tell you that marriage is terrible. Well, that's their experience. People who hate their jobs may tell you that the company you work for is terrible. Again, that may be their experience. People who don't like steak may tell you it tastes awful, but just because they don't like steak does not mean you won't enjoy it. Do not decide that your experience raising children will be negative based on someone's experience.

I heard someone say parents often wear exhaustion and stress from their children as badges of honor which can lead to having a negative mindset about parenting. Shift your mindset when dealing with your children to avoid playing the role of the martyr parent. You can find joy in parenting. You must!

Chapter 1

Parenting: The Best ~~Job~~ Joy I've Ever Had

"To change your life, you must change your mindset."
Brad Turnbull

In 1984, I was pregnant with my first child. One day, while getting my hair done by one of the older ladies in our community, Miss Susie, she shared life-altering words with me: "Make taking care of your children a joy and not a job." I didn't understand how those words would impact my life, but that was the best piece of advice I was given as a mother-to-be. That advice caused me to view parenting from an entirely different mindset. Any thoughts I had about parenting at that point were based on my observations of someone else's experience. My feelings were based on words and actions I heard or saw from parent-child interactions while growing up. Sometimes those words and actions were negative. I witnessed verbal abuse, children being cursed at, screamed at, and lives threatened. I witnessed physical abuse, children beaten with different objects, and emotional abuse, and I knew I did not want to be that type of parent.

On the other end of the spectrum, I saw very loving parents, parents that were kind, caring, and protective of their children. I always knew what type of mother I wanted to be because of my mother's example, but I don't think I understood how to become that type of mother. A single parent of eight, my mother was kind, thoughtful, easy to talk to, and patient. She loved her children and spread so much love throughout our small community. She had a great blend of love that included discipline in her everyday interactions with her children, which she learned from her mother. Her mother was also kind, thoughtful, easy to talk to, and patient. My mom, now 88 years young, continues to be a shining example of a loving parent. I grew up watching her, loving her, and longing to be the same type of mom.

As a child, I was very aware of things I wanted to do and be as a mom. When I would see different moms, I would take mental notes, but I never thought about how women become a certain type of mom. I did not realize that the mother I would become was more about the choices I would make. So, when

Miss Susie told me to make taking care of my children a joy and not a job, my ideals of motherhood began to click.

"Oh, I actually have a choice and a say in this," I would say to encourage myself.

Until that moment, I never realized I had a choice about the type of mother I could be, but her advice helped me realize I could choose to be a mom of joy, kindness, fun, discipline, and love. I could choose to deal with my children as a job and the frustrations of parenting or take pleasure and joy in every moment. The choice was mine, and I chose the latter. I realized that every day that went by was a day I would never have again to create wonderful memories with my children.

Taking care of children involves work, and I do not believe that the woman who gave me the advice insinuated motherhood is not challenging. Looking back, I think she spoke to a mother's mindset, the importance of deciding what type of mom I wanted to be, and the value of sticking with that decision. If I ensure my mindset is one of joy, then some of my frustrations may not be as overwhelming and, in some cases, may not be frustrating at all. I believe she was saying to never look at my children as a burden or an inconvenience, nor take on the children-should-be-heard-and-not-seen mindset, but to look at my children as the blessings God intended.

Children are God's blessings! They are not headaches, pains, or little monsters. God, the creator of the universe, said they are His reward: "Lo children are a heritage of the Lord, and the fruit of the womb is his reward" (Psalm 127:3).

A positive parenting mindset shift is needed.

Parents often find it easier to greet certain stages of their children's lives with joy. The newborn stage is usually the easiest to greet with joy because nothing is more innocent or sweet than a baby whose breath must be Heaven's perfume. Although, a colicky newborn can bring great stress to a new parent. But what about the toddler and teenage years? For quite some time, society has conditioned us to believe that those will be terrible times, commonly referring to a two-year-old's behavior as the terrible 2's. Imagine that – using the word "terrible" to describe a child's behavior at two years old.

Well, I am here to encourage you to find joy, not perfection, in all stages of your children's lives.

My entire life, I've heard horror stories about potty training, the terrible 2's, instructing children to clean their rooms, and teaching a teenager anything. As a young mother, hearing those stories can be frightening, especially the teenager stories. So, I chose to use the advice Miss Susie gave me. I started looking for ways to take pleasure in the little things and situations that often lead to frustration. Choosing to take pleasure even when circumstances were unfavorable was my choice, and I hope you choose to feel encouraged by the following parenting tips:

Tip #1: *Use encouragement for potty training success.*

Do not bypass this section if you have older children because you may have grandchildren one day, and this advice will help. Potty training can be a challenge, but many funny and amazing moments will transpire during the potty-training journey. Watching your child go potty for the first time is precious. It's one of those moments you realize that your child is growing up. It seems easier to magnify or focus on the challenging times of potty training. Right now, there are parents upset at a two-year-old that has not mastered the art of potting training. Why does this bring so much stress to parents? Is it because of the money that could be saved if their child were potty trained? Is it the messy diapers they have to clean? Or do parents choose to be stressed instead of enjoying the process?

Yes, you can enjoy the process.

Mom, your baby is growing and learning new things every day. With your guidance, love, and support, they will master many challenges.

Don't get me wrong. I understand the exhaustion of cleaning one messy diaper after another. But the fact that a two-year-old didn't make it to the potty in time has you mad, big mad, but why? They are only two. Poopy and wet diapers are not accidents but the natural process of potty training. Imagine if you were in your second year of med school, and someone expected you to perform heart surgery on a patient, but you had yet to learn how to do that. Now, people are mad at you. Does that seem fair? In time, however, you will be able to perform heart surgery, but it would be ridiculous for someone to expect that of you so soon. The same is true of potty training.

So, how can parents find joy in these moments? Let's refer back to Tip #1. First, a lot of encouragement is helpful for you and your child. Sharing encouragement helps parents get out of a negative, frustrating mindset and remain positive. It's hard to be negative in a positive environment. As the parent, you set the tone. You create a positive environment. Second, stay focused on small wins. Your child sitting on the potty or saying "potty" to let you know they need to go are special feats. Use a lot of positive reinforcement for your potty-training child. Third, remember that you were once a two-year-old. Treat your baby like you would have wanted to be treated. Remember this in all areas of your child's life. Treat your child like you would have wanted your parent(s) to treat you.

Being frustrated and upset with your child will not produce results any faster. Instead, your frustration may cause your child to become anxious. Every person over the age of two was once two, right? Barring medical or developmental needs, when is the last time you saw a ten-year-old or a 20-

year-old wearing a diaper? You haven't, and that is because they got it. Everyone eventually gets it.

Just remember that every child learns at a different pace. Some children are potty trained by age two, and others are not potty trained until three or four years old. Your child is not trying to frustrate you. They simply haven't figured it out. So, Mom and Dad, calm yourselves. Remember to breathe. This too shall pass, and your child will eventually get it too. (Smile).

Tip #2: *Use games to encourage little ones to clean up.*

The struggle is real when teaching a child to clean their room. I'm not sure if cleaning is innate to anyone, but it's especially not for children. Something I learned along the way to reinforce cleaning up was to sing a song. "Let's see if we can clean up before the song stops," I would cheerfully say, or I would create a game out of how fast my children could clean. Recently, I took this approach with my granddaughters (three and four years old), and it still works. I set the tone with excitement. We set the timer to see how fast we could pick up all the toys on the floor, and the girls were so excited as they quickly scrambled to "win" the game.

When the timer went off, we high-fived, and they jumped up and down. The youngest, while jumping up and down, said, "I won, I won." Truth be told, it was a win for me, too. They picked up the toys in one minute and nine seconds. The experience left them feeling happy, and I was stress-free. It was so much fun. You should try it!

At first, you will have to help your child(ren) because this tactic requires your participation, but it's a win-win because you are spending time with your kids. After a habit is established, they can do these tasks without you. James Clear, the author of *Atomic Habits,* shared, "A habit is a behavior that has been repeated enough times to become automatic" (2017).

So, how many times is enough?

That will depend on you and your child.

Remember to give the same praise and excitement when they clean their room alone. Also, it is easier to teach children how to clean their rooms if there is a designated place for their toys.

My daughter, who is now a mother, recently told me that she was having a tough time getting her children to clean up. She started using this tip to make the task into a game. After practicing for a while, all she must do now is say, "Ready, set, go," and her children run to clean their rooms.

I love it!

One day, on my way home from work, I stopped by to visit my grandchildren, and the first thing that my little ones said to me was, "Come look at our rooms!"

They were so proud!

Parents, Tip #2 is only for you. Decide if your child keeping their room clean is important to you. If not, that's okay. I would encourage you not to allow your child to destroy every room in your house, though. Excessive messes bring unnecessary stress to the entire family. Not having a designated play area in the house can pose a problem, too. This topic will be discussed in a later chapter. Remember that parents set the tone for their home, so set it with joy!

Tip #3: *Talk to your teenagers.*

If your children are young, read this section anyway because your children will one day be teenagers. Whether true or not, teenagers have a reputation for lying and being moody, defiant, aggressive, and unpleasant. Most people seem to believe that the teenage years are the worst of all. If you expect the teenage years to be the worst, they will be the worst. I enjoyed my children's teenage years, tough times and all.

When our children were young, we would sit at the table and have dinner together every night. Our table had six chairs, and we gradually became a family of eight, so as our family grew, so did the number of chairs. During dinner time, we would talk about our day. Once our children reached their teenage years, everyone's schedules were so busy that we did not have as many moments at the dinner table. Because our children were so close in age, life went into a tailspin once they grew.

Boy, we were busy!

We went from one sporting event to another, girlfriends, boyfriends, proms, jobs, school, church, and much more.

I enjoyed that crazy time when my children were transitioning between childhood and adulthood. Those were amazing years with special moments and trying moments. Yes, there were trying times. I knew challenges were bound to happen, yet a positive mindset helped me get through those times with strength and happiness. Please do not mistake a positive mindset for denial or obliviousness.

The teenage years are when familial relationships often change, and all the effort you've put in with your children begins to show.

If you have taken the time to create special relationships and bonds, it will show.

If you have found little time to spend with your child, it will show.

If your child feels that you are a safe place to share their failures and disappointments, it will show.

If your child feels they cannot talk freely with you, this is the season that it will become clear.

Parents will spend little time with their children when they are toddlers and feel confused why their teenager does not talk with them. Communication is a habit we must create in our children from day one. You must talk to your children when they are young if you want them to talk to you when they are older. This topic will be discussed in more depth later in Chapter 2.

Teenagers deal with so much. While this is not a biology book, we know that their bodies are constantly changing. From pimples to hair in new places, to voice changes, to new sexual feelings, every inch of their body transforms. On top of physical changes, there is constant peer pressure and new experiences like learning to drive, dating, and deciding if their future includes college, trade school, or no school at all. Internally, they are trying to navigate who they are, who they can trust, who their true friends are, and what they are to do with these emotions they don't understand.

As a parent, your role is especially important during these times. You not only deeply understand your child, but you also understand the challenges they will face because you were a teenager at one point. You've been through at least some of the things your teenager is experiencing.

One thing that separates us from our teenagers is that we did not experience teenage life in a pandemic nor with the same types of technology. In the palms of their hands, they have access to almost anything, good and bad, from porn to Bible verses. More importantly, regarding having information in the palms of our hands, how do you keep your children safe from predators? How do you keep them from being overexposed to information? Please think about the answers to those questions, and this will be discussed later in Chapter 7.

Technology in a teenager's life is a whole different world and beast. Social media often leads teenagers to believe they must have a perfect life, wealth, a flawless body, and designer clothes. That is a great deal of pressure for our young adults. So, have a little grace for their feelings, mood changes, and so forth. It is important to encourage and support your teenager while allowing them space to grow and discover, providing them a sounding board with an ever-listening ear.

As a mother, it is an honor for your children to talk to you on their tough days. It allows you to encourage them and builds trust because they know they can depend on you. One day, my 16-year-old daughter walked into my office and started to tell me about her day. She mentioned one negative experience after another. For her, it was the worst day ever. I knew that she was close to having a visit from Aunt Flo (her period), and I knew the toll that Flo would have on my daughter. I remembered how tough Aunt Flo was when I was a teenager. I fully understood what she was going through. As we talked, I knew I needed to find the delicate balance between being a safe place to vent and making her aware without being dismissive of what could be contributing to her heightened emotions. I told her I thought she was about to start her period, but she didn't think so.

After talking a little more, she had to return to school. Shortly after she left my office, I received a call from her, telling me she had started her period. I'm not sure why but we thought this was so funny and laughed hysterically. I was grateful for the opportunity to show my daughter that I would always listen and understand. I'm sure she wondered how her mother knew she was about to start. When we look back on that day, it is one of the funniest moments we shared and now frequently refer to, and it has become an inside joke.

Parents, more than ever, your teenager needs you. Sometimes, we think they need us less because they no longer need us to change their diapers or clothes. They no longer need us to hand-feed them, keep them from going into the street, or cook all their meals. Yet, they need us in different ways. We must be there to feed the soul and bandage egos, clothe their hearts, and nurse their pain. More than anything, we must be there to listen.

During the teenage years, especially, we want our children to hear our voices louder than any other, even when we are not around. For that to happen, we must spend as much time as possible talking to them and listening to them.

Does this mean your teenager will not make mistakes or bad choices?

Absolutely not.

Teenagers make bad choices sometimes.

When we were teenagers, we made poor choices.

I love hearing T.D. Jakes share the story of when his teenage daughter, Sarah, got pregnant and how he was willing to give up his ministry to support his child. Did becoming a teen mom keep Sarah from being everything she wanted to be?

No.

It seems as though her tough time helped her to be a better version of herself. Sarah Jakes Roberts is amazing, despite the decision she made as a teenager. She is wise and has helped many young ladies. Unlike the level of grace that T.D. Jakes showed his daughter, I have witnessed mothers reject their teenagers because of certain choices they made. Think about this: People will be furious at their teenager for getting pregnant, but later in life, they can't imagine life without their grandchild. (By the way, this is not an endorsement for teenage pregnancy). I remember taking a "note to self" to never reject my child because of a mistake.

Life is scary. Imagine being a teenager in a tough moment without the support and care of your family. Too many teenagers spend the toughest times of their lives feeling alone because they made mistakes and are ashamed, embarrassed, or too scared to tell anyone. Think about the hundreds of voices pulling on your teenager, voices enticing them to do wrong and to go down dangerous paths. They need to hear your voice louder and feel your support more, and that need is so great. In those moments, parents must be there like never before to offer wisdom and encouragement.

While you talk to and love on your infant and toddler, you are also setting the stage and foundation for talking to and loving on your teenager and adult, so set the stage wisely.

Some of my favorite memories of my teenage daughters were the times we spent shopping, laughing, riding in the car, and hanging out together. I loved helping them get ready for special events, proms, and banquets. When we would leave the hair salon, they always hated their hair. By the time we got home, it had grown on them. Well, most of the time. They looked like princesses, always beautiful. I loved when my daughters would playfully squabble about who got to sit next to me when we were at church or a sporting event. I always felt special. I loved watching them transform from teenagers to women. What beautiful, smart, and amazing women they are, and I am so proud.

I loved the times with my teenage sons, especially when I would walk up to them and they were surrounded by their friends, yet they would put their arms around me, kiss me on the cheek, and say, "This is my mom," never embarrassed my presence. My sons and I had special handshakes we would do when we saw each other. All their friends thought it was so cool. The cool thing about it was that they let me into how they viewed this world, and I enjoyed being in their world. I love watching them grow into men. What handsome, smart, and amazing men they are, and I am so proud.

I found joy in watching my children play sports – basketball, softball, baseball, cheerleading, and track – win or lose. I loved having someone else in the house that could drive. I loved when I would get a call saying, "Hey, Mom. My friends are going to the movies. Is it okay if I go, too?" I loved the sound of the many voices talking and laughing in the house. I didn't love the arguments between them, but that's life. I loved conversations after basketball games. I loved cooking for my children because they always made me feel like a great cook. I loved watching them have a good time with their friends. There are too many things to mention, but I loved those special times, and I love my relationship with each of my children. I loved and still love the holidays, especially Christmas. Their excitement on Christmas Eve was so sweet. Every year, on Christmas morning, I loved the look of anticipation and torture on their faces as they waited patiently while their dad read *The Christmas Story*. One year, my oldest son came into the great room, and he saw a big red bike. He jumped on the bike, assuming it was his, only to be told it was not. Boy, he was disappointed. At the time, it was not so funny to him, but now it's one of those memories that we laugh about at family gatherings.

There were many tears, laughs, and tough times, but the fun times outweighed the rough ones. While imperfect, teenage years were some of my favorites and could be some of your favorites, too. From a mother whose children are now adults, some of the mistakes that my children made when they were young are rarely mentioned or remembered at this point. I share that to share this: Do not fret over things that will not matter in the long run. The same is true of your mistakes as a parent; most are not mentioned or remembered.

One day, I rushed from work to go out of town for my daughter's basketball game. I arrived a bit late but caught most of the game. I thought it was a great game. Her team had won. When my daughter came out of the locker room, I congratulated her and told her she played well. She looked at me disapprovingly and said that she did not play well at all. She asked why I even came to the game because I made her nervous, and she plays terribly when I'm there. She was extremely disappointed with my presence. Even though her words hurt me, I realized she was not mad at me but mad because she didn't think she played well.

She walked away frustrated, and I walked away feeling a bit embarrassed because others heard her. She later returned to apologize, saying that she was disappointed because she heard scouts would be watching, and she didn't feel like she played her best. "Deep down, I knew I was taking my frustrations out on you," she admitted. She knew I would not return her anger with anger and would love her through it.

Just know there will be times when your children will be mad at you, but it's not always about you, so in those times, don't make it about you. They may say hurtful words, and while our children should respect us, they are humans and will make mistakes. This is not the time to get in a shouting match. Without getting angry or telling her that I am the mother and she better respect me, she figured it out herself. While it seemed like a big deal then, it was such a small moment that took place in our lives. But if I had made it a bigger deal, it would have been a bigger deal, perhaps something that would become a problem for our relationship later in life. Remember, unconditional love is quick to forgive.

As parents, we must also forgive ourselves. Once, two of our children had particularly important events happening at the same time. We had already planned to travel to our son's out-of-town event when our daughter's event was scheduled, which was also out of town. Financially, we could not make both work, so we attended our son's event because we had already made arrangements. This meant that my daughter had to attend her event alone.

Later, when my daughter called me from her event, she was crying. I was so sad that I was not there. She told me she understood, but I was so hurt that I let her be alone. I told her how sorry I was not to be there, and to this day, it makes me sad. I know I had to forgive myself, but "mommy guilt" is a real thing.

Parents, forgive yourselves.

We will not be perfect but must live and learn.

Two years later, I was in this same situation with another daughter, and I knew I had to be there for her, and I was. I would not let anything stop me. It was a tough lesson, but one I was glad to learn.

Find ways to make as many joyous moments as possible, even during challenging times. Life by itself brings enough depressive moments, such as the death of loved ones, natural disasters, wars, problems at school, and fights with significant others, to name a few. We do not need to add to that list.

Smile more, laugh more, and create more amazing memories to add to your child's memory bank. When you are gone from their lives, all your children will have are memories. What do you hope those memories will look like?

For a few seconds, put on your superhero goggles to see through time. It's 20 years from now, and your adult children and their families have gathered for Christmas. Play the scene in your mind.

What's the atmosphere?

How's the conversation going?

Are there wonderful memories being shared?

Is there laughter in the room with one funny story after another? You know, that thunderous laughter that explodes in the room, that side-splitting laughter that draws you even closer together?

Why is this familiar to you?

Because you experienced those moments. You lived them. You experienced the pure joy that words cannot explain and only laughter is needed. Laughter reveals the bond created in those memories that make your family whole and that bond that will exist for a lifetime.

If a close family is what you hope for in the future, you must start now. If you expect a peaceful, fun-filled environment when they are adults, your home cannot be one of negativity and stress when your children are young. You want your family to be excited about getting together instead of feeling excited to leave. In retrospect, now that my children are adults, this was the best advice I received – to find joy in being a parent and not allow the stresses of life to steal that joy. So, if you want your children to have memories of parents that made traveling through this life a joy more than a job, you must start as soon as possible.

I look at parenting as a scale. There is joy on one side of the scale, and on the other side is a job. As much love as I have in my heart for my children, I know I've made many mistakes, yet I want the balance to tip in favor of joy at the end of each day, week, month, and year. When our children are grown and look back on their childhood, they will recognize that there were tough times, but the scale tips in favor of joy. Every day, parents should be mindful of putting joy in their child's joy basket:

- Say "I love you" and give hugs to add joy to their joy basket.
- Read to them before bed and give goodnight kisses to add joy to their joy basket.
- Walk hand-in-hand to add joy to their joy basket.
- Be patient when your children struggle with their homework to add joy to their joy basket.
- Have a day off to take your child to lunch to add joy to their joy basket.

Every day, visualize yourself adding to your child's joy basket. Be aware of what has gone into this basket at the end of the day, especially whether their joy basket is full. If the basket is lacking, seize the following day to change the narrative.

Looking back, I wish I had captured more memories through pictures and journaling. For parents raising children in this tech age, capture every moment. I heard my daughter say that she takes pictures of her son and sends them to an email she created for him. I love this! I would add to that to also send messages about special moments in your child's life and funny things your child said because you will forget so many of them, trust me. When your child is an adult, they will have many special moments to share with their families.

People tell you that time goes by fast. As a mother with adult children, I must say this is true. Slow down, enjoy the moments, and make taking care of your children a joy, not a job.

Chapter 1

At a Glance

Are you working to ensure your child's joy basket is full every day?

What is one thing that frustrates you about being a mom that you can try to find joy in?

Every day, you must:
* Say "I love you" often to your child(ren)
* Hug your child often and stay in the hug
* Remember how much you love being a mom, even during tough times.

The goal is to focus on finding as much joy as possible in being a mommy and making sure your child laughs often and has a joyful childhood.

Chapter 2

Quality Time

"Your life requires your mindful presence in order to live it.
Be here now."

Akiroq Brost

Because life is busy, you must make spending time with your children a priority. While you may not have quantity time, you can have quality time. If you want your children to talk to you when they are older, spend time talking to your children when they are young. Develop a habit of talking to your children, not about them or over them but to them. Think about how much time you spend daily talking to your children. I'm not talking about statements like "clean your room," "pick up your toys," and "go take a shower." That is not conversation. Instead, ask open-ended questions that require responses.

"How was your day?"

"What was your favorite moment so far?"

"Did you learn anything new today?"

Think about this: If you work outside the home, you go to work for eight hours a day, but you must get dressed for work, right? That could take 30 minutes to one hour. If you drive to and from work, the commute could take anywhere from 30 minutes to two hours, depending on where you live. Then, factor in that your child sleeps eight to 12 hours, depending on their age. So, of your 24-hour day, how much time do you actually spend with your family? For some, only a couple of hours. I wake up at 6:30 am to get dressed for work. I drive to work and work eight hours, only to get home a little before six. If I had young children in my home, they would be in bed by eight. That would mean I would only have about two hours to spend with my children and husband daily. There is cooking, eating, and bathing, even some laundry and other chores to be done during that time. We have two days for the weekend, but there is always so much to do. The point is time is valuable. So, the amount of time you spend with your children is limited. Please be aware and learn how to maximize time with your child.

Tip #1: *Involve your child in what you do for them.*

Involve your child with cooking, cleaning, running bath water, laundry, and shopping. Yes, those tasks may take longer, but you are spending time with your child and teaching them simultaneously. You will be surprised how much a small child can learn and help you. All the while, they love the experience because they are spending time with you. One of my greatest joys is watching my three-year-old granddaughter help her mother cook. She has her own apron, and her mom gives her small tasks to do. Try to involve your child in at least one activity weekly until it becomes a part of how you do things, and be sure to find joy in this time together.

Tip #2: *Set aside time, weekly, to be alone with each child.*

It may only be 15 to 30 minutes, but this allotted time will make each child feel special and strengthen your bond. I would keep the time consistent, so your child will know they always have time with you. You will be surprised how much your child will look forward to this special time together. Be mindful of wasting time. Time is something we can't get back, so be intentional about spending time with your child(ren).

Parents are often baffled why their teenagers do not want to spend time with them. Possibly, they never established a habit of spending time when they were young. Think about how you laugh and talk with your friends and how much fun you have in their presence. Talk to your children with that same joy, love, and laughter. You may have to put your phone down, get off the computer, be present, and listen. Make sure to look them in the eyes while talking to them. Make this a daily habit. I will mention this again – if you do not talk to your children when they are young, they will not likely talk to you when they are older.

Although life is busy, stay present. Cell phones, TV, and friends can be distractions from your children. The problem with busyness and distraction is that we don't realize time passes while life is happening. We think we are multitasking – talking on the phone, playing a game on the phone, and spending time playing with our children – but are we? Someone or something is being cheated of time, and usually, it is your child.

My youngest son used to call me out on this. He would say, "Mom, you're not listening to me." My daughter calls it the "mommy tune-out." I would look in his direction, nodding my head, smiling, and saying yes, yet not hearing a word he was saying. This was something I had to improve. The times that he called me out, I apologized and tried to do better. When he called me out, I could not be angry because he was telling the truth. Well, I guess I could have been angry and just pretended he was lying. But no, I had to be better and do better. I did not want my son's memories to be about the times he tried to talk with me but I was too busy doing other things to pay attention to him.

Spending time with children should not feel like continuous labor. Times of joy should outweigh stress, anger, being overwhelmed, and anything else. I remember hearing a young mother on vacation say of her children, "I can't wait to get these kids back to their babysitter."

Note to self: Do not take your children on vacation and not enjoy them.

There she was on vacation with her beautiful children but didn't seem to be enjoying the very reason for vacationing (creating great memories with family). Instead, she was in a rush to get her children back to the babysitter. She could have been having a tough day, which certainly happens, but it caused me to think of how many times I had the perfect moment to create a special memory with my children but allowed my stress or frustration to steal the moment. This is something to think about, especially because we can't go back to that time.

Tip #3: *Prioritize cultivating a relationship with your child.*

Friends will come and go, but you will always have a connection with your child. These little people become your forever friends. Isn't that the type of relationship worth investing in?

I had friends who I thought would be in my life forever who I no longer talk to or talk to once in a while, but guess who remains in my life every day? My children, who are now adults, that's who. I was always one of my children's biggest supporters, and now they are my biggest supporters, and their love is unconditional. These familial relationships have been worth the investment. Giving your family the best of you is of the utmost importance. Some people give their jobs their best or friendships their best, and when they spend time with their children and family, they get what is left over. People will go to work and be amazing, focused, and productive but come home to be rude, unpleasant, and unkind.

There are two mothers that are amazing stars that I would like to contrast, Lucille Ball and Diana Ross. I loved Lucy! (No pun intended). She is a legend, hilarious and entertaining, and made growing up in the 60s and 70s fun while watching her show. If you were old enough to enjoy the humor of Lucille Ball, then you loved Lucy, too. I grew up watching the funniest lady alive and thought how amazing it must have been to be her daughter. But when you hear her daughter talk about her mother, you hear a different story. In an interview with Joan Rivers, Ball's daughter said that her mom was a control freak, did not connect with her children, and did not know how to have a relationship with her kids. I also heard the daughter say something very sad. As her mom was dying, she thought that her mom realized she had difficulty connecting to her children because she was lonely when she reached the end of her life. Of course, her mother parented and loved them the best she could and set her children up financially but did not have a great relationship with them. Hearing her daughter speak about her relationship with her mom was not what I expected.

Then, there is Diana Ross, a legend, mother of five, world-renowned singer, and actress. She was an artist I grew up listening to, along with all the Motown greats. I didn't become a huge fan of Ms. Ross until my freshman year of college in 1979. I bought a new album of hers and was sold.

I recently heard an interview with Oprah and Diana and her children. I was amazed! Diana was giving her energy to the world, all the while establishing amazing relationships at home with her children. You could tell by the way her children spoke about her that she is an amazing mother.

Oprah stated that she heard Diana does not like making movies, to which Diana explained that she does enjoy making movies, but what she doesn't like is the waiting around, being in the trailer, and doing makeup when she could be home with her kids.

If you have ever been to a Diana Ross concert, you know she connects so well with the audience. You feel that she loves you, and I speak from experience. She is amazing at connecting to millions of people, yet she connects and shines her light in her home, as it should be.

Moms, it's not how well you connect to the world or how bright your light shines outside your home. Yes, that is important, but what matters most is when you take the time to establish necessary relationships with your children. Whether you are a working mom or a stay-at-home mom, are you taking steps to have an amazing relationship with your children?

Spending time with my family is my happy place. I have great friends, and I love spending time with them, but nothing compares to when my family is in one place with one heart.

Looking back, I wish I would have spent time teaching my sons how to cook and clean, and I wish my husband taught my girls how to change a flat tire and basic auto skills. We raised our children with traditional roles. When I think about it, it's ridiculous that I didn't teach our boys to cook. Who will cook for them? Well, they both have had to cook for themselves for many years now. Neither is married, but if they were married, it would have been nice for them to cook for their families. They have made many calls to their sisters and me for instructions on cooking a meal. They are pretty good cooks now, but it has taken them a while to learn.

The same goes for my girls. What if they are alone and have a flat tire? Who will change it? Yes, we have roadside service, which is great, but basic car knowledge would have been beneficial, too. I'm still a very traditional woman, though, because I believe the man should always have to kill the spiders... period!

I also wish I had talked more with my children about sex as it was age-appropriate. It's interesting because I thought I talked to them often about this topic, but when I spoke to them while writing this book, they said I talked about it with them but more in passing. I don't remember being embarrassed, so I don't know why I did not have this conversation more, but I know that even if you feel your children are in a sheltered environment, which we were, they will hear about sex. They will hear about it from friends, in school, at church, and on TV. It's everywhere. Do better than

I did. Talk with your children about sex to ensure they receive accurate information.

Chapter 2

At a Glance

How aware are you of spending quality time with your children?

Calculate how much time you spend at work and work-related activities (getting dressed, driving, working, and decompressing, plus how much time your child sleeps). Determine how much time you have daily to spend with your child.

What is your scheduled time, daily and weekly, to spend with your child(ren)? Tip: I have written this time down and shared it with my child to help me stay true to this commitment.

Plan special time with your child just as you plan date nights with your partner and girls' nights with your friends. The goal is to put in the work necessary to have a great relationship with your children.

Chapter 3

Setting Expectations

"Train up a child in the way he should go, and when he is old, he will not depart from it."

Proverbs 22:6

The second-best advice I was given was not to expect my children to do things I had not taught them. The mother that shared this advice referenced it by saying, "Don't allow your children to climb all over your furniture at home and then go to church and expect them to sit quietly on the pew." Children do not automatically know how to do certain things, especially sit still. That is why, biblically, parents are admonished to teach their children. With time comes experience, and with experience hopefully comes wisdom. Please enjoy these tips, as they proved beneficial in my home.

Tip #1: *Teach your children at home to do what you expect of them when they are in public. If not, don't be mad at your children for doing the unexpected.*

What are your expectations when you take your child to church, the store, or a doctor's appointment? Whatever you expect, teach. Teach your child to do those things at home. If you want your children to know how to sit still, you must work on this with your child at home. Start as simple as saying, "Let's see if we can be quiet until the timer goes off," or play the quiet game. If you want your children to pick up toys in their room, you must teach them. Yelling from the other room to clean up is not training but stressful and a joy sucker. Threatening them to do certain things is not training. You need to go into their room, and with a great attitude, show them how to do it, over and over. That's training!

Early in life, I spent a few years as a kindergarten teacher. One year, I had so much fun with my class. Besides teaching the fundamentals of reading, writing, and arithmetic, I taught the importance of obedience, hearing my voice, and responding, the same lessons I taught my children. We practiced daily. If I turned the lights off one time, that meant to be still. We would practice being frozen and listening for instructions until the lights came on. Although we had so much fun, a lesson was learned. We learned how to quietly walk through the hall, pretending to be little mice so no one could hear us. That year went well, and the class had a blast. Little did I know that training would one day be the very thing that kept us all safe.

One chilly morning, a staff member came into my classroom to tell me there was a fire in the building. About 20 children were playing on the classroom floor at the time, and toys were everywhere. I'm sure an alarm went off, but I don't remember because I was focused on getting the children out of the building. I immediately went to the light and turned it off one time. In a soft voice, I said, "Boys and girls, line up in front of me." All the children immediately stopped playing and formed a line. Then, I opened the back door, which was an exit that put us immediately outside. While walking the children away from the building, I could see that smoke had already filled our classroom. Just that quick!

That day, I gained a new understanding of the importance of training children. Once I got them outside, I counted them over and over. They remained quiet and orderly, which allowed me to ensure their safety and confirm their presence. Those children were amazing! I shudder to think of what would have happened that day if I had not spent time teaching those little ones how to obey quickly.

My point is this – do not expect your children to do things you have never taught them. If you have never taught your children to sit still, it's unfair to expect it from them. It is unfair to take them to a restaurant or an event and be upset with them for acting as children do. If you want your children to be polite and respectful, show them how to be polite and respectful. If you want your children to be kind, teach them kindness by their interaction with you and how they see you treat others. "Please" and "thank you" have been replaced by "give it to me," "I want it," and "now." Children do not know any better than what they are taught.

I read a post on Facebook that stated, "If you have children, remember this: when you are finished with them, the rest of the world has to live with them, so please teach them respect." So, teach what you expect. We cannot throw our children into this society and hope they will magically be respectful, kind, and obedient. We must teach them.

Teaching our children what we expect also makes it easier for others, such as teachers, coaches, and peers, to deal with them, too. Remember that teachers do a job most parents would not consider doing, such as taking care of other people's children for seven hours a day, five days a week.

Tip #2: *Have realistic expectations according to your child's age and ability.*

One day, I was studying in the library. Yes, I was the mother going back to college in my 50s, sitting in the front row, listening to every word. There was a young mother in the library with her 18-month-old baby. This young mother kept nagging her baby to be quiet. She repeatedly said, "Be quiet" and "shh," so much so that she began to annoy those around her. I went up to her and asked if she wanted me to take her child outside to play while she studied. She said no. While I don't blame her for not letting a stranger watch her child, I felt so sorry for a baby that was expected to sit quietly in the library. We cannot expect children to do what they have never been taught or do not have the ability to do. Parents often hold children to unrealistic standards they cannot attain.

Is asking an 18-month-old to sit still for a couple of hours in a library a bit unrealistic?

Absolutely.

Sometimes, parents think that children should not get angry, have attitudes, or have bad days—all things adults do and feel daily, especially throughout the workweek. We want our toddlers to exhibit self-control by not running in the house, but do we exhibit self-control when we lose our cool because our toddler will not stop running? Who should have self-control, the four-year-old or the 30-year-old? We expect a four-year-old to have self-control, but we don't? Interesting…

Many moons ago, I worked at a preschool. A boy and girl were sent to my office because the little boy punched the little girl. As I talked to them, trying to find out the truth, both children told me that the little girl bent the little boy's finger, so he punched her. So, I called their parents. The mother of the little boy wanted me to spank him for punching the little girl. (Yes, there was a time not that long ago when schools spanked children). I understood what his parents were trying to teach him, that boys should not hit girls, or that perhaps he could have responded differently, but there was an unrealistic expectation for the little boy in this situation. My response to these parents was no. So, I talked with both children and sent them back to class. My reason was that if someone unexpectedly bent my finger, that I, as an adult, could not say if I would have enough self-control not to react and maybe throw a punch. So, that is an unrealistic expectation for a child.

I am also reminded of when my grandson played soccer for the first time at three years old. There was an expectation from my athletic family that he would automatically be great. We are athletes, and my grandson could already run fast. Well, his soccer experience was hilarious. He was more interested in running around with his friends and getting gummies and snacks after the game than playing soccer. In fact, I'm not sure if he ever followed the ball. The funny thing is I don't know why there was an expectation of greatness because he had never played. No one had taken him to the backyard to teach him the basics of soccer.

Simply put, he was no David Beckham. My family soon realized that expecting a child to be great at something they had never done or had never been trained to do did not make sense. We look back at that time and laugh. The video of my grandson on the soccer field, running in the opposite direction of the ball, chasing his friends with no clue where the ball was, is priceless and brings so much joy to us all.

Also, remember that external sources can set expectations of what's acceptable. Be particularly careful not to overexpose children to TV, especially programs you don't want your children to learn from. If the TV program shows children talking crazy to their parents and cursing, and you don't want your children to think that behavior is acceptable, do not let your children watch those shows. Instead, expose them to wholesome TV shows where a lesson can be learned. Of course, that means many shows may be off your list, and as your children get older, maybe you can add other shows for them to watch, but by that time, expectations should already be set for what's acceptable. It may be more difficult to find shows that teach your child a lesson, but it is worth the effort. Other parents may have an opinion about how you raise your children. Mom and Dad, you are the parents. Others, including family, may not understand the choices you make for your children. Everyone may not agree with you, but you must do what is best for your children.

Looking back, I wish I had allowed my children to express themselves more openly without feeling like I had to manage their emotions, but rather giving them the wisdom to manage their emotions instead. I was quick to correct them when they were angry. I saw anger as dangerous, which it can be, but anger is a normal emotion when managed.

Chapter 3

At a Glance

List what you expect of your children.

Confirm that your child has the ability to do those things. Confirm that you have taught your child how to do those things. Do you have unrealistic expectations for your child(ren)? If so, what are those expectations?

The goal is to set your expectations based on your child(ren)'s abilities and to find joy in your responsibility for teaching your child.

Chapter 4

Yell Less

"Remember, anxiety is contagious - and so is calm."

Debbie Pincus

A friend of President Alexander Hamilton once suggested for him to talk less.

My suggestion? Yell less.

A simple question to ask yourself is, do you want your child to talk to you when things are not going well in school? When they are sad? When their friends are mean to them? If the answer is yes, yell less. If you want to find more joy in parenting, stop yelling. Yelling is not good for you, and it serves no benefit to your child. This does not mean you will not have serious conversations with your child.

Yes, you will need to be stern, but yelling is not the way to lead those conversations.

Yelling should be reserved for emergencies, such as your child doing something dangerous, about to harm themselves, or not hearing you in a crowded place. If you use yelling for everyday communication, your child will not be moved when you raise your voice in a dangerous situation.

When my son was small, he was playing in the front yard with his siblings. As I was videotaping them, and he started to walk toward the street. I noticed and called him back to the yard, but he did not respond. So, I dropped the camera and started running to him, screaming his name. I'm sure I scared him terribly. Needless to say, there are times we may have to yell, but those times should seldom be.

When we yell at our children constantly, we teach them not to talk to us. Who wants to confide in someone who cannot effectively communicate, and you know they will just yell at you? If you tell your boss something at work and their response is to raise their voice at you, I assure you, you will not want to talk to them again. You may even quit your job, and if not, you will find ways to not talk to your boss or circumvent them. Similarly, our children may find ways to avoid us or not talk to us. While they may choose not to speak to us, they may choose to talk to someone else. They may talk to their friends, their friends' parents, or someone that gives them bad advice. They may also "quit" us by not letting us engage in many parts of their lives, especially as they grow older. If you desire to be the one your child confides in, you must stop yelling. Instead of yelling, take a deep breath, share wisdom, and provide encouragement.

If you yell every time your child does something wrong or makes a mistake, you're telling them mistakes are unacceptable. Making mistakes is as natural as breathing. There isn't a person alive that has not made one mistake. Often, we yell at children for the very things we did as a child and sometimes still do as adults. We are who we are partly because of the lessons we learned from the mistakes we made.

Another problem with yelling is that you teach your child not to respond to your regular voice. Children should stop doing things because we said it, not because we are screaming. We should always be able to get a response out of a child, not only when we yell. If I had needed to rely on yelling in my classroom to get my students to line up during the fire, I hate to think what the outcome might have been.

Before yelling, do a self-check.

Are you yelling because you are out of control?

Are you having an adult tantrum because of a lack of self-control? Often, that is the case.

Ask yourself if yelling is how you want to teach your child to respond to you.

Can you get a response from your child without yelling?

Is yelling helping your child?

If the answer is no to at least one of those questions, it's time to rethink your strategy and try something different. When you are angry and yelling at your child, stop and look at the fear in their eyes. People who yell all the time, unless drill sergeants, lack self-control and do not know how to govern their own spirit. The Bible says, "A soft answer turns away wrath," which may indicate that a harsh answer stirs up wrath (Proverbs 15:1).

Studies on WebMD suggest that yelling at kids can be just as harmful as hitting them (Sturiale, 2021). In this two-year study, effects from harsh physical and verbal discipline were found to be frighteningly similar. A child who is yelled at is more likely to exhibit problem behavior, thereby eliciting more yelling. This is a sad, tragic cycle. Speak health to your children with your pleasant words: "Pleasant words are as a honeycomb, sweet to the soul, and health to the bones" (Proverbs 16:24).

Note to self: I will not make a habit of yelling at my children. Yelling is a terrible habit and shows a lack of self-control. It is my responsibility as a parent to nurture my children.

Nurture is a powerful word. Look at how Merriam-Webster defines the word nurture: to help (something or someone) to grow, develop, or succeed; to take care of (someone or something growing or developing) by providing food, protection, a place to live, etc. (2021).

If you ever properly planted something, you know you watered it and ensured it received the right amount of sunshine. You protected your plant from the cold and harsh elements because you knew those things could destroy your plant. You may have talked and sung to your plant, too.

Why?

Because you wanted to create an environment where it could grow. You worked hard to create an atmosphere where your plant not only grew but thrived.

What environment have you created so that your child grows and thrives?

Well, your child is like a plant. This environment should not include constant yelling and screaming. If you find yourself losing your cool, try the following tips:

Tip #1: *Take a timeout.*

Yes, I know we use timeouts for children, but it's perfectly fine to recognize that you are losing your cool and need to cool off. After cooling off, have a conversation with your child about whatever upset you. Speak wisdom to your child!

Tip #2: *Be quick to examine yourself.*

Although you are the adult in the parent-child relationship, you are still growing. Self-examination is important for continued growth. Be honest with yourself. Are you upset with your child, or is something else driving your anger? If the latter, do not take it out on your child.

During my senior year of high school, I came home from school and told my mother that I had smoked marijuana that day. It probably wasn't the first time, but this time, I knew a relative saw me. I was sure the person who saw me would go home and tell her mother, and that mother would tell my mother. So, I wanted my mother to hear it from me first. As soon as Mom arrived home, I met her outside and told her the story. She looked at me and began to share with me why it was not a good choice. Not once did she yell or become angry. And because of the way she spoke with me, I knew I could always be honest with her, even if I had messed up. As a parent, you want this kind of healthy relationship with your children. You want your children to talk to you about anything so that you, as a parent, also have the opportunity to offer wisdom and guidance or just listen. As parents, we often forget that we did similar, if not the same things, too. Of course, we do not want our children to make those mistakes, but if the mistake is made, how can we help without alienating them?

Yell less.

I read an encounter on the National Alliance on Mental Illness (NAMI) Website between a client and a therapist. Please take a look:

"The problem with verbal abuse is there is no evidence," Marta shared. She came for help with a long-standing depression.

"What do you mean, lack of evidence?" I asked her.

"When people are physically or sexually abused, it's concrete and real. But verbal abuse is amorphous. I feel like if I told someone I was verbally abused, they'd think I was just complaining about being yelled at," Marta explained.

"It's much more than that," I validated.

"The problem is no one can see my scars." She knew intuitively that her depression, anxiety, and deep-seated insecurity were wounds that stemmed from the verbal abuse she endured as a child.

"I wish I was beaten," Marta shared on more than one occasion. "I'd feel more legitimate."

Her statement was haunting and brought tears to my eyes.

Verbal abuse is so much more than getting scolded. Marta told me that there were many reasons her mother's tirades were traumatizing:

1. The loud volume of her voice
2. The shrill tone of her voice
3. The dead look in her eyes
4. The critical, disdainful, and scornful facial expression that made Marta feel hated
5. The long duration—sometimes her mother yelled for hours
6. The names and insults—you're spoiled, disgusting, and wretched
7. The unpredictability of that "flip of the switch" that turned her mother into someone else
8. And, perhaps worst of all, the abandonment.

Being frequently yelled at changes the mind, brain, and body in a multitude of ways, including increasing the activity of the amygdala (the emotional brain), increasing stress hormones in the bloodstream, increasing muscular tension, and more. Being frequently yelled at as children changes how we think and feel about ourselves even after we become adults and leave home. That's because the brain wires according to our experiences—we literally hear our parents' voices yelling at us in our heads even when they're not there. To read the rest of the story, visit www.nami.org.

Tip #3: *Apologize if you cross the line.*

I don't believe that most parents want to be abusive to their children. Unfortunately, as stated earlier, according to the National Children's Alliance, most child victims are abused by a parent. The person that should be nurturing, loving, and protecting their child the most becomes the abuser. Often times, it's a result of the parent's inability to control their own anger. The problem with being angry and yelling is that you easily lose control. Ecclesiastes 7:9

teaches, "Do not be quickly provoked in your spirit, for anger resides in the lap of fools."

For too many years, parents have given themselves a pass when they lose it. It is not okay to verbally abuse children. Constant yelling is abuse, and parents often do not offer an apology. It is not acceptable for a parent to berate children by calling them out of their name and using language that should not be spoken to children, yet the adults, the mature ones, do this. Making excuses while holding a child's feet to the fire for their behavior is not acceptable. As adults, we must take responsibility for our actions. If we cross the line, we must apologize.

No more excuses.

No more hiding behind the fact that there are no visible scars from verbal abuse.

There are scars, effects, and pain. If you want to find joy in being a parent, the yelling must stop.

Looking back, I believe now more than ever that yelling is not a healthy or effective way to parent a child. I don't remember my mother ever yelling at me. Thankfully, her decision not to yell positively affected how I parented because I did not yell at my children. So, if you are a yeller, think about how behaviors like this can get passed down from generation to generation. If not for your children, please stop yelling for your grandchildren's sake because your child may adopt the same communication tactics and yell at their children and continue the toxic cycle. How you communicate with your children is so important. It creates the environment for them to not only grow but thrive, so please stop yelling.

Chapter 4

At a Glance

You understand the damage yelling at your child can cause. Instead of yelling at your child, take a timeout to cool off.

I know you do not want to hurt your children. Please understand that yelling at them can hurt them. Yell at sporting events and yell at the TV, but do not yell at your children.

The goal is to not yell at your children because of the fear, anxiety, and trauma it can cause them. I want you to have a great relationship with your child, and yelling can harm that relationship.

Chapter 5

Remove the Blinders

"Remember you are not managing an inconvenience. You are raising a human being."

Kittie Frantz

Be willing to accept the truth about your children. Do not wear blinders. I recently heard a mother say that her three-year-old child would not lie. I raised six amazing children, and they would all lie at that age. My response to that mother was perhaps your child may be so good at lying that you can't tell the difference. Yes, your child will lie, not because they're "bad" but because they are human.

If your child is never corrected for lying, they may grow up to be a liar.

If your child steals and is not corrected, your child may grow up to be a thief.

If your child is a bully at home and is not corrected, they may be a bully at school.

According to Stomp Out Bullying, bullying is learned in the home, sometimes from a bullying sibling or parent. Bullying is a learned behavior that can be unlearned, but if we ignore it, it will not stop (2005). Seize every opportunity to teach and train. When your child falls short, that is not the time to be angry, ashamed, or embarrassed. Everyone must be taught. It is fairly normal for children to push their limits. If they get away with it, they will try it again. If corrected, they might not.

Early in my teenage years, I started noticing parents that thought their children could do no wrong. Unfortunately, those teenagers were some of the sneakiest kids I knew. When their parents were informed about their child's antics, the parent would say, "Not my baby." I remember making a note to self as a teenager to be truthful about my children. Pretending certain behaviors do not exist will not make it go away, but it can cause the behavior to escalate. And because the behavior is ignored, no wisdom is being offered, nor training or teaching to help children grow. If you are honest about the behavior, at least it gives you a chance to help your child(ren).

Some children will misbehave at school, and when the parent is called for support, they become upset with the teacher instead of their child. We should know if our children are capable of the things teachers tell us.

When my son was in preschool, I received a call from his director telling me that he had cut a piece of a little girl's hair. When I arrived at the school, I asked him why he did it. He had told the teacher that the little girl had her hair on his desk, and he asked her to get it off. She didn't, so he cut it. He told me that same story. The school staff didn't seem to think it was a big deal. He wasn't sent to the office or put in timeout. There were no consequences for his behavior. While I didn't fully agree, he was only four, so I thought maybe it wasn't that big of a deal. Plus, the little girl's mom who worked at the school thought it was funny, although I'm sure it probably wasn't funny to the little girl. So, I didn't discipline my son either, even though deep down, I knew I should have.

Well, guess what happened?

He did it again.

One day, my daughter was resting on the sofa, and when she woke up, she thought something was crawling on her shoulder, so she screamed. Unfortunately for her, my son had cut off her braid. By ignoring his behavior, I made it easier for him to do it again.

I also remember when one of my daughters got mad in a basketball game and threw the ball at another player, hitting her in the head. Her coach sent her to the locker room for the rest of the game.

Should I have been mad at the coach for taking her out of the game?

No, because although I understood things become heated on the court, her actions were unacceptable. And although I did not like seeing my daughter get pulled from the game, I liked her actions less.

Those are the times when we should not ignore our child's behavior but use it as an opportunity to teach.

No one on this Earth is always right. When your child is right, you must stand with them and support them, but if they are wrong, they are wrong and saying they are right will not make it so. Check out the motto from my high school graduation in 1979, which is applicable to this day:

We do the absolute best we can,

The best we know;

And will continue

To do so until the end.

If the end proves us right,

Nothing else matters.

And if in the end, we are wrong,

Ten angels swearing that we were right

Will not make it so.

I often share that philosophy with my children. If you are right, Mom will support you, but if you are wrong, I will support you but never cover your wrong. There is no joy in living a lie. There is joy in the truth!

Do teachers and adults cross the line?

Yes.

As a child who suffered injustice at the hands of adults, I know that parents must be careful. There have been times I had to stand with my child instead of an adult. I remember when one of my girls was in her senior year of high school. She was an amazing basketball player, a defensive stopper. She was always given the task of guarding the best player on the opposing team, and she was always up for the task. When the end of the year came around, she was so excited because she knew she earned defensive player of the year for her team. I had been around basketball all my life and understood what was required to be the player of the year. I had been to most of the games that season and saw her defensive greatness. I, too, expected that she would be the player of the year. I remember sitting with her in the ceremony when her coach gave it to another girl that was not the team's defensive stopper. I could tell my daughter was hurt, but she kept a great attitude throughout the ceremony. I had been through this myself, so I wanted my daughter to know I understood.

This kind of thing can be frustrating for a teenager or any child because the choice seems obvious, and we expect adults to do the right thing. So, I made sure my daughter knew I thought she was the defensive player of the year. While that coach gets to make a choice he deems suitable, I can still support my child.

There are times adults mistreat children, and there are times when adults lie on children. So, try to find out what is true and stick with the truth.

We must teach our children to respect authority, but they also must talk to us and let us know when they feel the authority has crossed the line. We must be a safe space for our children to share openly about an adult and feel certain that we will not always take the adult's side. I remember my mother standing up for me against an adult who accused me of something untrue. I remember how that made me feel. I felt so loved to know my mom stood for what was right and did not choose a relative over me.

When my son was in third grade, he told me that his teacher did not like him. First, no child should feel that an adult does not like them. He said that she would not call on him if he raised his hand and that she was really tough on him. While I wasn't sure what "really tough on him" looked like, I knew I needed to talk to her. So, I went to see his teacher and expressed how he was feeling. I heard his side, but I wanted to hear her side because there are always two sides. Someone said there are two sides and the truth. That sounds about right. I don't think she realized how she was coming off to my son.

After my conversation with her, she talked with him. He said things improved. I asked him about this situation recently now that he is an adult. He said he realized that the teacher was trying to help him be better, but as a child, he thought she did not like him. He said she was still tough on him, but he understood what she was trying to accomplish because she communicated with him. He said, "It's crazy that as a child, I thought she didn't like me. She was a great teacher!"

If I had just taken my son's word and been angry at his teacher, I would have been wrong, only to find out later that he had a misunderstanding. So, please try to find the truth in every situation. We can help our children better when we deal with the truth and when they know we will stand for what is right.

Teach, train, and do not make excuses for your children. Remember the old saying – an excuse is the next cousin to a lie. So, making an excuse for your child's behavior is just as bad as lying to them or for them. Deal honestly with your child and show them integrity by your interactions with them, their teachers, and others. Protect them, cover them, love them, and walk in truth toward them. Never let an adult take advantage of your child. Stand with your children when they are right. When they are wrong, use it as an opportunity to teach, train, and share wisdom.

Tip #1: *Always search for the truth.*

Watch your reaction when something is said about your child. If it is true, this allows you to work with your child instead of being angry with the person that gave you the information.

Tip #2: *Don't ignore the truth. Unfortunately, it will one day bite you in the backside if ignored.*

The truth has a way of surfacing, so it is best to accept it from the beginning. We have been given a great responsibility to be an example to our children, to teach and prepare them for this world and their future. We cannot effectively do this when wearing blinders. President Franklin D. Roosevelt said, "We may not be able to prepare the future for our children, but we can at least prepare our children for the future." Parents, the future fast approaches, so take the blinders off, and let's get them prepared.

Years ago, I heard a fable:

A boy had been caught stealing and had been condemned to be executed. He desired to see his mother and to speak with her before execution. When his mother came to him, he said, "I want to whisper to you," and when she brought her ear near, he nearly bit it off. The bystanders were horrified and asked him what he could mean by such brutal and inhuman conduct. "It is to punish her," he said. "When I was young, I began stealing little things and brought them home to Mother. Instead of punishing me, she laughed and said, 'It will not be noticed.' It is because of her I am here today."

Looking back, I believe honesty is not only the best policy but the only policy. Honesty is not just an option but a necessity in dealing with our children.

Chapter 5

At a Glance

I will be honest about my children to help them be the best they can be.

I will not assume that everyone is wrong and my child is right. I will search for the truth.

The goal is to deal truthfully with my child, knowing that my focus is finding as much joy as I can in being a parent and making sure my child has a joyful childhood full of truth.

Chapter 6

Silence, Rest, and Self-Care

"To be a good parent, you need to take care of yourself so that you can have the physical and emotional energy to take care of your family."
Michelle Obama

Adults understand the importance of silence. Sometimes, it's good to sit quietly and reflect. There is so much going on in the world, and we are often in constant motion from sunup to sundown. We need a few minutes to sit quietly and breathe. There is nothing like taking a few minutes to be still and silent and do a little "soul care," as Pastor Sarah Jakes Roberts calls it. Also, as adults, we understand the importance of rest. My body tells me when I need to rest. When I listen to my body, I ward off sicknesses by allowing my body to rest. If I do not listen to my body, I find myself sick. Children have not learned to listen to their bodies. So, we must teach them the importance of silence and rest.

Hear me out on this one. There are times when children should be silent, even if for a few minutes a day. Again, it is not a children-should-be-seen-and-not-heard mentality, but more so that children need silence as adults do. We used to call it "quiet time." We used the "quiet" game to teach children this concept. This provides a refresher for their body and mind. Secondly, it helps children understand that there are times and places not meant for running around and screaming. Being quiet for a child is not something they will automatically do; it must be taught. The following tips teach the importance and implementation of quiet time.

Tip #1: *Have your child sit for a few minutes every day with a book. Call it quiet time.*

Do not make this a punishment. Make it the most amazing thing they get to do. We want children to learn the pleasure of sitting quietly, maybe looking at a book, maybe with a pen and paper, or just sitting and thinking and being creative. Teach your children to sit quietly at home with a book every day for a few minutes, stating that this is their quiet time. Grab your book and read, too. TV and phones should be off. That way, when you transition outside of the home, perhaps in the doctor's office, you can give your child a book and say, "It's quiet time," and your child will understand what is expected. For small children, start with a few minutes. If your children are older, you can start with 15 to 30 minutes. If you never taught them to embrace quiet time, it will require consistency.

Tip #2: *Make sure your children get plenty of rest.*

If your child is continuously screaming, crying, and unhappy for large parts of the day, there may be a simple solution. I'm not a doctor, but I can tell you that most children do not get enough sleep. Getting enough rest is a vital part of a child's physical and mental development. Getting proper sleep is like eating a balanced diet. There is a reason children become cranky when they are tired. As adults, we become cranky when we're tired, too. Lack of sleep can cause concentration and behavior issues in children.

I met a young mother with two children, ages three and four. From our first few encounters, I could tell she was exhausted with a capital E. Her children were so sweet but stayed in motion. As we talked, she started telling me about her home life. She said her children get up early every morning and do not go to bed until late every night, anywhere between ten and midnight. I asked how long they nap and at what time, and she said they do not nap. I was shocked. I didn't think toddlers could go that long without sleep, which kind of explained their behavior.

I suggested putting them down for a nap to give her time to regroup and give their bodies time to refresh. She said her children would not take a nap. So, I asked her to put them down at the same time every day and to turn off all stimuli, like electronics. She said she would try it. The first day I was at her house, she tried to put them down, but they played for the entire time yet stayed in bed. I asked her to do it at the same time the next day. She did, but her children did not nap. By the third day, both of her children took a nap. This was a game-changer. They started napping daily, too. Three days is not necessarily the magic number. You may have to try this for more than three days, but be consistent.

Then, I asked her to consistently put her children to bed every night at the same time (around seven or eight), employing the same nightly routine – bath, read a book to them, give them a bit of water, and so forth. She did it, and her children started resting.

Inconsistency affects children.

Children long for guidance.

When there is none, they do their best, which is not the same level a parent could provide.

Naps are our best friends. I love how refreshed my children felt after a good nap. If they went to bed cranky, they would wake up refreshed and sweet. In our society, we burn the candle on both ends. Children are involved in many sports and extracurricular activities. They go to school and have hours of practice after school. They travel and play sports at such young ages. Parents must be the "sleep patrol," making sure their children get plenty of rest daily.

Have you ever seen a child that is so tired but "fights" their sleep? They don't know how much their bodies need sleep, but as their parent, you know.

Parents who let their children go all day, and then around five in the afternoon, the child can't help but fall asleep, are only punishing themselves. If your child takes a nap at five, they will more than likely not be ready to go to sleep by seven. Now you, the parent, must be up late with your child. This vicious cycle leaves everyone cranky, especially the parents, which makes you unable to find the joy of parenting. Regarding the important topic of sleep, John Hopkins Medicine reports the following:

Sleep is an essential part of everyone's routine and an indispensable part of a healthy lifestyle. Studies have shown that kids who regularly get an adequate amount of sleep have improved attention, behavior, learning, memory, and overall mental and physical health. Not getting enough sleep can lead to high blood pressure, obesity, and even depression (Dawkins).

John Hopkins Medicine also reports that "establishing a consistent bedtime routine is important (Dawkins). Ideally, the routine should start at the same time every night. As soon as the sun goes down, start to "wind down" the household by doing the following:

- Dim the lights.
- Stop the use of electronics/screens at least an hour before bed.
- Limit caffeine.

- Take a warm bath.

- Do a quiet family activity such as reading a short book.

- If your child wakes up during the night, walk them back to their room with as little commotion as possible.

- Set a wake-up time for when the child can leave their room. The child can play quietly until that time if desired.

- Be consistent when establishing good sleeping patterns with children. Children's bodies need rest.

Tip #3: *Practice self-care.*

If you are on a plane, and the plane experiences difficulty, you should put your oxygen mask on first and then help your children. In other words, if you don't take care of yourself, you cannot take care of others.

I remember when my children were young, and I started having blood pressure issues. My doctor told me that if I didn't take care of myself, I would not be around to care for my children. So, I made the needed changes. That doctor's visit was my first indication that I needed to take care of myself and practice self-care.

You must practice self-care. I'm not saying spend all your free time on yourself; that is not self-care. That is selfish. You must take care of yourself physically, mentally, and spiritually to care for others. Being in a chaotic world with a chaotic life is exhausting, but if you allow yourself time for self-care, you will find more joy in parenting.

Something I would do daily is encourage my children to enjoy quiet time so that I could have a few minutes to myself. Starting when they were babies, if they were asleep, I would rest, too. As they got older, each child had their own quiet space to get a book or choose to be quiet, and we did this daily for 30 minutes. The younger children would nap, but the older children would have quiet time with a book or not; it was their choice. This was my time to regroup, refresh, and renew. It was only 30 minutes, but it was enough for me. If you allow yourself to go all day without a break, you will soon find yourself "losing it," yelling more, and being impatient. You must take time to recharge. Finding time to care for yourself may be difficult, but it will be worth it. If you have the option of getting a trusted babysitter or occasionally taking a day off work while your child is at daycare or school to take care of yourself, do it.

I read this the other day on Instagram, and I love it – "Sitting outside of your house in the car is self-care."

That is the truth!

If you're a single mom, it may be more challenging to have "me time," which is why it is extremely important to teach your child how to have quiet time. You may have to enjoy self-care time while your child has quiet time.

A big part of why I enjoyed my time with my children is that I saw being a mother as my calling, so I practiced self-care. When I was a young mother, no one ever told me about the importance of self-care. I never labeled what I was doing as self-care. I just found time to rejuvenate. I tell people that I don't remember feeling any different or overwhelmed when going from one child to six, but that is because I practiced self-care, probably not great self-care, but some self-care. Give your child the best you. To do that, you must be the best you. Practice good self-care.

A couple of things can take away from your rest and cause you to feel overwhelmed, one of which is a messy house. Take a look at the following insight regarding a messy house.

- Not having a place to rest in a clean environment is a stress trigger. Your home is a refuge, or it should be...

- Allowing children to destroy your home is another stressor. Having a designated place for toys is important. If toys are on the floor in every room, this could cause stress. Instead, opt to create play areas. Adults understand the importance of play in a child's life and do not want to keep a child from playing. We want them to play hard. After your children are done playing, teach them how to put the toys in their place. As stated early, make clean-up time a game, encouraging your children to see how fast they can pick up the toys. Making small adjustments can take your level of anxiety down and help you feel less overwhelmed.

- Be sure to have a designated place to eat. Have you ever seen a small child walk and eat at the same time? How much food gets in their mouth and how much on the floor? Allowing your children to eat everywhere can cause stress. I've observed many children that do not sit to eat. That's a parent's choice, but do not be upset with your children for leaving food from one end of your home to another and drinks spilled on your floors in different rooms. Just know this can be the cause of some of your stress. If you want to lower your stress level and create an environment where you can enjoy your home, teach your children to eat in certain spaces. It's okay to recognize that your child is not the only person in the home, so you have to make this work for everyone involved. Children need their play areas, and you need a clean room to go to for peace. Both needs can be met.

In the beginning, teaching your children to pick up toys or eat in designated spaces will be extra work, but I'm telling you that you will be so glad you did it in the long run. It would be better to take the time upfront to teach than to deal with the extra stress throughout the years. Even though you are raising children, you are still growing and must protect your peace.

I heard someone say, "We wear our tiredness as a badge of honor." We are exhausted, but why are we always exhausted? Take care of yourself, and you may not be so tired.

Looking back, I truly believe finding time for myself helped me not feel overwhelmed with six children. I'm so glad this generation stresses self-care.

Chapter 6

At a Glance

Make sure your child gets enough rest and times of silence.

Do not allow yourself to feel guilty for practicing self-care. Self-care is needed for you and your children.

The goal is to focus on helping your children get adequate rest to be their best and for you to practice good self-care to help you not to feel drained or overwhelmed.

Chapter 7

Children Need to Feel Safe

"For God hath not given us the spirit of fear; but of power,
and of love, and of a sound mind."

2 Timothy 1:7

This world can be a scary place – the pandemic, racial unrest, school shootings, mass murders, natural disasters, death, the "boogie man," the shadow in the closet, and the news. The news alone can be very scary to a child. I remember being young and hearing about guerilla warfare. As a child, I thought gorillas were killing people, and I feared they might come and kill me.

Know that the little ears in your house hear what is being said, and more importantly, absorb what is felt. Your children hear your fears, so we must be careful not to overwhelm them with adult information, only sharing what is age-appropriate. Your child does not need to know every detail of the COVID pandemic, but they certainly need safety information. Parents must create an environment where their children feel safe, especially in these times.

When our children were between the ages of five and 15, we had quite the experience with a tornado and high winds. We were in our high school gym, watching a pick-up basketball game when one of the player's pagers kept going off. Pagers were used in pre-cell phones times, so for those that do not know what a pager is, it's a wireless device that receives and displays alphanumeric messages. The message was from his wife, asking him to call home. We knew it was storming outside because we could hear and see the rain, but we had no idea how bad the weather had become.

When he finally called home, his wife told him that a tornado was headed toward us. So, my husband closed the gym, and we headed home. We could barely drive because the wind was so strong. As we got home and turned on the TV, we immediately saw Gary England on News 9, telling everyone to take cover. Well, there were eight of us plus one visiting child. So, my husband took the older children to the back closet. I took the younger children to the bathtub and covered the area with a mattress. I led my children in prayer, trying not to show my fear. At one point, it sounded like a train was traveling over our home. It was such a scary night.

The next day, we went for a drive in the neighborhood. The gym we were in was destroyed, along with parts of my children's school. We were thankful that the man whose wife paged him finally answered her message. We thank God for our safety that night. As this story demonstrates, life brings enough fear of its own. So many things that happen are out of our control. We can't control natural disasters, but what we can control, we should—that is why I stress that we should not bring unnecessary fears to our children.

When I was 13 years old, my 16-year-old brother was killed in a car wreck. Even though I was 13, I felt as if I was about seven because coping with his death was such a heavy experience to endure. Prior to my brother's death, I received a call from a boy that went to school with my siblings and me. He said, "Soni, Orelious has been in a wreck."

I turned to my older sisters, who were home from college, and told them what he said. Shortly after that, the phone rang again, and I regretted answering the call. "Soni," he said again, "Orelious is dead." That call changed my life, and it took me years to recover. Days following, the newspaper headline read, "Freak Accident" about my brother's death. I didn't understand that they were not calling him a freak but the accident a freak. A few days later, I sat at his funeral in our high school gymnasium. There were so many people in attendance, and I vividly remember the sounds from the room. People were groaning and screaming from a place of pain. I would look up and see young people crying, and I hear those sounds to this day, which remind me of a haunted house. During my brother's funeral, I stayed near my mother, keeping my eyes on her because she was the only source of comfort in the room. She would look at me with a very solemn look and lift her chin ever so slightly to encourage me. I would catch my breath and accept the strength she imparted to me.

Unfortunately, during the days following the funeral, fear took over me. I was in a constant state of fear for my life, feeling that I was dying or about to die. My mom would allow me to sleep with her when I needed extra comfort. Sleeping next to her was the only safe space in my world. I don't think I ever told my mother how afraid I was, and I don't think I understood the magnitude of my fear. Children have fears; even though they may not articulate their fears, they are still very real.

Recently, I told my mom how I had felt, and she did not know how scared I was at the time, but she had unknowingly made me feel safe by allowing me to be in her space. When I was about 26 years old, I conquered that fear of death by the grace and Word of God.

Losing a sibling, grandparents, or anyone close to you can be traumatic. Your children may experience the death of a classmate, close friend, family member, or well-known figures like the death of Kobe Bryant, Michael Jackson, or Whitney Houston. News about our country going to war and mass shootings, especially at schools, are terrifying for children. Inclement weather, tornadoes, earthquakes, and floods can be terrifying, too. Children may also fear things like animals, insects, the dark, and needles. Be aware to check in with your children. They may not be able to express their fears, but it is possible that they have them, and those fears might manifest in different ways. Death is difficult for adults, so imagine the toll it can take on a child. Parents should be the safe space for their children. Be the place they can come to when they are afraid or don't have the words to express their feelings. Do not bring extra pressure on your children. Again, life itself brings enough stress, and we don't want to add to their stress levels.

When I became a mother, one of my daughters had the same battle with fear. It was especially important she felt safe and never felt alone. I wanted her to know I was always there for her, no matter what time of day or night, no matter her age. I wanted her to know she could depend on me to give comfort and be a listening ear. I remember the comfort I received lying next to my mother, so I wanted to give that same comfort to my daughter.

The age of your children (from toddlers to teenagers) does not matter because there will be times throughout their lives that they deal with fear. We always want to be there, be present, listen, and give comfort. Take the time to talk, embrace, pray, and empower children with God's Word and do not hesitate to seek professional help for your children. Whatever their fear, empower them. The Boogie Man and the shadow in the corner are real to your child. Help them overcome and empower them against all fears but do not ridicule or bully them into being brave.

On the topic of helping children be brave, we must remember not to argue in front of them, as it can bring anxiety for our kiddos. Arguing in front of children can also cause fear. Disagreements happen, but please find a way to disagree amicably. You must decide not to argue in front of your children. We have all seen movies of children sitting in the corner horrified while their parents argue. Those are not disagreements but arguments. Be the example for your children, showing them that you can respectfully disagree. Importantly, never use your children to hurt another human, especially during legal battles and custody hearings, and do not say negative things about the other parent. Parents should never use their children to get back at the other parent or hurt grandparents or in-laws. It's so shameful how children are put in between adults.

Fear can cripple our lives as adults, so imagine what it does to children. Anxiety, depression, and mental health issues are widespread in much of our world. Children have these same battles. Be aware, help your child, and seek professional help if necessary.

Make sure your child is not exposed to scary programs and videos through TV, tablets, or cell phones. Be sure to watch for commercials that come up during games and videos they watch. I recently played a game on my phone, and the commercial that came on was an ad for a video game. The setting was a prison, and the prisoner was shooting and killing the guards. Then, what looked like a large monster came out of a room and killed the prisoners. The commercial was gruesome! If a show does not align with your morals, values, and beliefs, do not expose your children to it. Children can take on real fears just from watching the wrong thing. There are some shows I can't even watch as an adult. I remember the effect *The Exorcist* had on my teenage sister. She was petrified to a level that only people who have experienced that type of fear would understand.

According to Healthychildren.org, the following are suggestions that many parents find useful for their children with fears and phobias.

- Talk with your child about their anxieties, and be sympathetic. Explain that many children have fears, but they can learn to put those fears behind them with your support.

- Do not belittle or ridicule your child's fears, particularly in front of peers.

- Do not try to coerce your youngster into being brave. It will take time for your child to confront and gradually overcome their anxieties. You can, however, encourage (but not force) them to progressively come face-to-face with those fears (Shelly Vaziri Flais and American Academy of Pediatrics 2018).

Every year, when our children were young, we would take them to Arbuckle Wilderness, a drive-thru safari park. Arbuckle Wilderness also had a petting zoo and an area with rides like bumper cars. There was one little water ride where the children would get in a tube and float in the water. One of our daughters, who was three years old at the time, got into the tube, was floating, and started crying, but when we got her out of the tube, she was fine. There was nothing physically wrong with her, but she was so upset yet could not articulate what was happening. So, I just tried to comfort her. Sometimes, parents get mad in these situations because they don't see any reason to cry. It wasn't until years later that I found out why she was crying. We were looking at some pictures from that trip, and she told us that the wall of the water ride was painted with a large frog, and she thought the frog would eat her. That's a real fear! I would have never thought that friendly-looking frog would bring my child so much fear, but it did.

Parents, you may not know why your child is upset or fearful. You may not understand their tears. Just know there is a reason which they may not be able to articulate. Whether your children's fears are real or perceived, they are fears. Do not be angry with them. Be gentle, kind, and understanding.

So, when your children are fearful, try these tips regarding easing your child's fears.

Tip #1: *Address fear talk such as "I'm afraid to..."*

Make talking about fears easy. Talk it through, and empower your child.

Tip #2: *Pray with your child and give comfort through the Word of God.*

My favorite scripture to share with my children was and still is 2 Timothy 1:7: "For God hath not given us the spirit of fear but of power, and of love, and of a sound mind."

I would be amiss if I didn't mention adverse childhood experiences. Sure, children will recover from skinned knees or a tumble, but childhood trauma can have lifelong consequences. A 2019 report confirmed that experiencing traumatic situations as a child puts the child at risk for lifelong health effects. The 2019 study expanded on the link researchers first identified in the first adverse childhood experiences (ACE) study, conducted by the Centers for Disease Control and Prevention and Kaiser Permanente, over two decades ago. That research identified the link between ACEs (potentially traumatic connected events that occur before a child reaches 18) and negative health and behavior outcomes later in life ("Unwrapping the Link between Childhood Trauma and Health" 2021). If you are not familiar with the ACE study, please take some time and research it. It looks at these three categories of ACEs:

- Abuse: Physical, emotional, and sexual
- Neglect: Physical and emotional

- Household dysfunction: Mental illness, a mother treated violently, divorce, incarcerated relative(s), and substance abuse.

There are decades of research linking ACEs to an increased risk of developing chronic diseases and behavioral challenges, including obesity, autoimmune disease, depression, and alcoholism. New research has also uncovered a correlation between ACEs and an increased risk for prescription opioid misuse ("Unwrapping the Link between Childhood Trauma and Health" 2021). Not surprisingly, multiple ACEs put individuals at a greater risk for negative outcomes, including poor school performance, unemployment, and developing high-risk health behaviors, such as drug use. These high-risk behaviors account for nearly 50% of the increased risk of negative consequences associated with ACEs ("Unwrapping the Link between Childhood Trauma and Health" 2021).

Please note: The points addressed in the ACE study are not things that children are exposing themselves to but that adults are exposing children to. When are we going to stop being okay with the harmful ways in which we deal with children? Why is the way we deal with children not considered an epidemic? The more adults I deal with that have major issues in their lives usually come from parents who were detached, took discipline too far, abused a substance, and had unmanaged mental illnesses. Dr. Robert Block, the former president of the American Academy of Pediatrics, said adverse childhood experiences are the single greatest unaddressed public health threat facing our nation today, and I happen to agree.

Keeping Children Safe from Predators

Predators come in all shapes, sizes, ages, colors, ethnicities, and religious backgrounds. Recently, I heard on the news about a 78-year-old man accused of sexually assaulting children in his neighborhood. The people in the community knew him as a "good man" that always helped kids. How often do we hear these stories on the news about people that have been convicted of sexual assault of children? All the while, the people in the neighborhood think that person is a great person and has no clue of their dark secrets. So, how do we protect our children from predators?

I knew of a story where a young girl whom we will call Ann, maybe about 12 years old, wanted to spend the night at her friend's house. However, Ann's mom would not let her child spend the night with this friend. She told her daughter that although she knew her friend's mother, she did not know the father. Ann did not understand but accepted what her mother said. Years later, it came out that Ann's friend's father was "grooming" his child for incest. Unfortunately, most people that take advantage of children are relatives or someone close to the family that the child has been taught to respect. People who take advantage of children by inappropriate touching, fondling, or rape are usually people the child knows.

I was horrified by this as a young mother. My children were not allowed to sit in men's laps, among other things, because of my fears, regardless of how close the person was to our family. Having heard stories of inappropriate behavior from people who were close to me fueled my fears. Please look at the facts from the Young Women's Christian Associate (YWCA) about child sexual assault:

- A common myth is that child sexual abuse is perpetrated by strangers and pedophiles. However, most people who sexually abuse children are friends, partners, family members, and community members. About 93% of children who are victims of sexual abuse know their abuser. Less than 10% of sexually abused children are abused by a stranger.

- Children are at heightened risk for sexual violence. Nearly 70% of all reported sexual assaults occur to children ages 17 and under.

- One in four girls and one in six boys will be sexually abused before they turn 18.

- About 12.3% of children were age ten or younger at the time of their first rape/victimization, and 30% were between the ages of 11 and 17.

- The younger the victim, the more likely the abuser is a family member. Of those molesting a child under six, 50% were family members. Family members also accounted for 23% of those abusing children ages 12 to 17 ("Young Women's Christian Association" 2021).

The following topic is also incredibly sad; at times, we must protect our children from other children, especially children who have been exposed to certain things. Those children may expose your child to the things they have experienced. If they have been touched or fondled, they may touch or fondle other children. It is so sad for a child to lose their innocence. I wish we could protect all children from predators. We must be vigilant when children are in the presence of adults and vigilant about supervision when they are in the presence of other children. That does not mean not letting your children play and be a child; it just means that you have to do the extra work. We cannot protect our children from everything; however, we must try.

So, how can we protect children from adults or other children who prey? Unfortunately, we must talk about this. There are a few precautions parents can take:

- Talk to your child and ensure they feel comfortable telling you anything.

- Keep an eye on children where strangers have access to them, such as parks and indoor play areas.
- Parents cannot assume anyone is safe. Do your due diligence to get to know who will be in your child's presence.
- Talk to your children in detail when they return from a friend's house.

Looking back, as a young mother, I had many fears about my children and how to keep them safe. For a period of time in our lives, my children were not allowed to go in the backyard and play without my supervision. I only allowed them to go to the homes of people if I knew both parents. I tried my best to empower them against any person who may become a predator, even if that predator was a relative or family friend. Abuse was a huge fear for me because I knew people who had been molested. It wasn't until my mother told me to put my children in the hands of God and trust Him because I can't be everywhere at all times. When I found myself being fearful about them, I would pray for them. So, yes, teach them and train them, but ultimately, we must trust Jesus.

Chapter 7

At a Glance

Make your home a safe space for your children.

When you notice that your child is fearful, talk about those fears with them.

Be mindful of saying things that may cause your child to feel fear.

Only share age appropriate information with your child.

The goal is never to shame children for their fears but to talk and be a safe place for them when they are fearful.

The goal is for children to be nurtured and cared for and never abused physically, verbally, or sexually. Let us protect our children as a momma bear protects her cubs.

Chapter 8

Speak Positively and Never Compare

"Death and life are in the power of the tongue."

Proverbs 18:21

Words are powerful.

Watch the words you speak over your children, and do not compare your children to others.

Our world is framed by the words we speak over ourselves or that others have spoken over us.

When we speak negative words over our children, and they agree with those words, a self-fulfilling prophecy can manifest. If you tell your child they are dumb, even though they may be very smart, your child may not show how smart they are. Some might think that no one would call their child dumb, but it happens.

Years ago, a man told me that throughout his childhood, his father would tell him he was a bum.

"Guess what I became in life?" he asked me.

He said he became a bum, and it took him years to overcome what had been spoken in his life.

Not only should we be careful to never speak negative words over our children, but never allow others to speak negative words over them either. The damaging effects can yield the same negative results.

When I was a kindergarten teacher, I had an experience with a child and their parent that will forever remain etched in my mind. The student, five years old, was joining my class. I was excited to have him in my class because I had met his mother, who also worked at the school, and we quickly became friends. When I spoke to his mother, she was discouraged about her son's ability to learn. Imagine being discouraged about your child's education at five. She was told very negative things about her child's ability to learn and how far he was behind others his age. While visiting with my student's mom, she told me she was concerned that her son would not be able to attend college when he grew up. She really thought something was wrong with him. She told me that she would hide her son's yearly standardized test results and not discuss them with the other mothers because she did not want them to know his struggles. This tells us how damaging words can be. If she buys into the narrative others have spoken about her child, she may pass those negative feelings, words, and thoughts to her son.

No one should pass judgment about a child's ability to learn, especially not a five-year-old. Why speak negatively about a child's ability to learn? Every child learns at a different pace and has different learning styles.

As I started to work with her son, I noticed he did not like a noisy room. He was very studious and did well if everyone in the room was reasonably quiet. If not, he would ask the other students to be quiet. If the room became too noisy during work time, it became a bit of a challenge for him. So, my classroom was perfect for him. There was structure during work times, but the work times were riddled with lots of play-to-learn activities. So, I quickly realized that this child had been labeled the D-word; however, he merely learned differently.

During my first conference with his mom, I showed her his writing.

"Did you help him with this?" she asked in disbelief of the worksheet.

Her child excelled that year, mostly an A student with a B or two.

The following year, his mother asked if her child's first-grade teacher would be a good fit. I assured her that the teacher would be a good fit because she ran her classroom similar to mine.

The young man who had others speak negatively over him early in his life will soon graduate from college with a degree in engineering. His mom and I are still good friends and remain close to this day. We often laugh about how she felt during those early years of his life.

Words are powerful.

Have your child tested if you suspect learning and developmental delays or if your child's teacher suggests so, but be careful about accepting words from non-professionals with a mere opinion.

I am a firm believer that every child can learn, especially if the right atmosphere is created. I also believe that if I could teach a child to sit for a period of time, I could teach them anything. Sometimes, what others label as learning disabilities are behavior issues or require a different teaching style. Parents, be careful of the words you speak over your children and the words you let others speak over your children.

As a child, I was skinny with sandy reddish-brown hair. I had a large gap between my front teeth, so I covered my mouth when I smiled. When people talked about how skinny I was or my gap, I internalized their words. I can't say that those words were spoken maliciously, but I took them that way. There were times I did not feel pretty, but my mother always told me I was beautiful. Besides my mother, a lady from our community, Mary Alice, always said the kindest words to me. By the time I got to high school, I felt pretty most days, even though very little changed about my body, and I still had a gap between my teeth. If I didn't have adults speaking positively in my life, I wonder if I would have taken on a negative self-image. I am now 60, and I still remember that kind lady's words and how those words made me feel. Those words helped shape my self-image and helped me to see my inner and outer beauty.

I encourage parents to not only speak kind words to their children but to all children. Your words may be the only kind words a child receives that day. You may be the reason that child takes on self-respect or self-acceptance. Be a part of the community that helps fill the joy basket of all our children. Dr. Hyder Zahed, a scientist, author, and speaker, once said:

Words are singularly the most powerful force available to humanity. We can choose to use this force constructively with words of encouragement or destructively using words of despair. Words have energy and power with the ability to help, to heal, to hinder, to hurt, to harm, to humiliate, and to humble (Zahed 2014).

When my children were small, I was particular about the words I spoke over their lives, including something as simple as changing the words to "Rock-a-Bye Baby":

Rock-a-bye baby

On the treetop.

When the wind blows,

The cradle will rock.

When the bough breaks,

The cradle won't fall.

Because Jesus watches over baby,

Cradle and all.

I always thought it was so bizarre to sing about a baby falling from a tree, and I decided I would not sing death or an accident over my child. Don Miguel Ruiz, the author of *The Four Agreements*, shared a powerful sentiment regarding words:

The word is not just a sound or a written symbol. The word is a force; it is the power you have to express and communicate, to think, and thereby to create the events in your life. You can speak. What other animal on the planet can speak? The word is the most powerful tool you have as a human; it is the tool of magic. But like a sword with two edges, your word can create the most beautiful dream, or your word can destroy everything around you (Don Miguel Ruiz 2008).

Your words can destroy everything around you, and that includes your children. To this day, I am incredibly careful about the words I speak in my life. I remain careful not to frame my world negatively because I might experience what I say.

A young minister asked his wife how she was doing, and she said, "I'm tired." A bit of time passed, she looked at him and said, "Well, actually, I'm not tired. I don't even know why I said that."

Basically, we confess a lot over our lives with our words. We repeatedly say how tired we are and then are shocked when we feel tired, or we say how sick we are only to find ourselves sick. We're framing our world, word by word. This concept is at the very basis of man's existence. Over the years, I've told my children that they are intelligent, amazing, and wonderful. I don't believe I ever called one of my children bad. I don't think that word ever came out of my mouth or should ever come out of your mouth. I taught them about disobedience, but being disobedient is not bad. "You are bad" is a terrible thing to speak over a child. Look at some of the words associated with bad:

* Substandard
* Poor
* Inferior

- Inadequate
- Dreadful
- Awful
- Terrible
- Worthless
- Abominable
- Atrocious
- Deplorable
- Hopeless
- Diabolical
- Inept
- Lousy
- Pitiful
- Godawful

Telling your child they are bad is like telling them they are deplorable, diabolical, and worthless. Is that the message you want to send to your child about how you feel about them? Choose to speak words of wisdom to your children, something to give your children strength for days and years to come. Something you spoke to them in their younger years could profoundly impact their lives forever. Your child will quote you and your wise sayings – "I remember when Mama used to say…" or "I remember when Dad used to say…."

When I was a teenager, Jimmy Carter was president, and my mom had told me something about President Carter's daughter. She said, "You're just as good as her. You're not better than her. She's not better than you, but you're just as good as her." I felt empowered to know that my mom believed I was just as good as the president's daughter. After almost 50 years, I still remember those positive words she spoke to me.

My Uncle Lee would always tell us, "Don't take no wooden nickels," and while I didn't know what a wooden nickel was when I first heard him, I understood the message when I figured it out. I think about his statement from time to time, which helped me not settle for something fake, ultimately helping me through life.

Speak life and let your children know they will be everything God said they could be. Tell them they will be amazing, somebody this world is glad they were born in, and somebody that leaves an imprint on this world. Tell them they are a world changer. Start framing their world when they are little bitty babies. Start speaking over their lives even while they are in the belly, as you hold them in your arms, and when you breastfeed and bottle feed. Create the habit of speaking into your kids' lives positively.

Death and life are in the power of the tongue.

Choose life.

Give your child a mantra to live by and speak words to your children that bring joy in their hearts and your home. And remember not to compare your children to others.

Your child is unique! They can be born in the same family with the same blood, have the same last name, yet be different. They have different looks, gifts, talents, personalities, and temperaments. They should never be compared to one another or anyone else. President Theodore Roosevelt once said that comparison is the thief of joy. To find joy in parenting, do not compare your children to their siblings or other children. *Being the Parent,* a company that supports parents through the journey of pregnancy and parenthood, states that comparing your child includes the following effects:

1. Stress

2. Lowers self-esteem

3. Lowers self-worth

4. Shies away from social situations

5. Builds carefree attitude

6. Suppresses talents

7. Distance from you

8. Fosters sibling rivalry.

To ensure your child does not experience the negative effects of comparison, consider the following tips:

Tip #1: *Don't make children feel insecure by comparisons.*

When my children were young and in the presence of other children, I was very aware to never make comparisons. "Why can't you do it like this child," "why don't you fix your hair like this child," and "why don't you act like this child" are statements that should never be spoken.

Adults must never make their children or other children feel less than by comparing them to others. Some adults like to put other people's children down to make their children feel better or show favoritism. One child feeling left out or put down is unacceptable. Some parents brag about their children in the presence of other children just to make them feel poorly. Yes, adults do these types of things.

Do not be that adult that treats other children poorly. Parents, do not allow other adults to treat your children differently. Some adults will not discipline their children yet discipline or correct someone else's child. Parents, don't do this. Do not discipline others' children but let your child get away with what you chastise others for doing.

All children are God's children and should be treated as such. Matthew 18:6 states that it is dangerous for us to offend a child. So, it is our duty and responsibility to care for children. Lord, help us protect and love the little ones in our lives and never make them feel less than by comparison.

Looking back, I realize I took the scripture "death and life are in the power of the tongue" very seriously (Proverbs 18:21). I did not speak negatively about my child and did not allow others to, either. Children believe what you tell them, so speak life!

Chapter 8

At a Glance

Be mindful to never compare your children with their siblings, friends, or anyone else.

Tell your children about the strengths you see in them. Build them up.

Speak words to your children that make them feel good about themselves. Speak to their future and teach them how to speak to their future. Our worlds are framed with our words. Mother Teresa once said, "Kind words can be short and easy to speak, but their echoes are truly endless."

The goal is to speak words that build up your children, telling them how amazing they are and speaking life, not death. This will help you have a great relationship with your children and help you find joy in parenting.

Chapter 9

Discipline Is Not About You

"Train up a child in the way he should go; even when he is old, he will not depart from it."

Proverbs 22:6

I saved this chapter for the end of the book because there is so much controversy about the topic. Something that is not up for debate is that we should never discipline children in anger. Anger can be an untamed emotion, proven to be extremely dangerous. People make poor decisions in anger that they would not ordinarily make. People have hurt children in fits of anger and rage. If you want to find joy in parenting, never discipline in anger. You cannot take back physical damage, not to mention the mental damage that can last a lifetime. Even in non-physical discipline, be careful not to discipline in anger. Yelling, screaming, and levying extreme punishment is unacceptable. Timeouts are useful, but like anything else, they lose their power when overused. Anything in this world that is abused will lose its power.

We need food to live, but it becomes maladaptive when abused.

When you abuse your car, it won't run properly.

When you abuse your money, you will be poor.

When you abuse your home, it won't be your sanctuary.

When you abuse your time, you won't be productive.

When you abuse our planet, wildlife, and sea animals, our planet will deteriorate.

Sometimes, we discipline our children because they made us mad, embarrassed us, got on our last nerve, or because we needed to let off steam from our terrible workday, all of which are the wrong reasons. This bears repeating: People make poor decisions in anger that they would not ordinarily make.

Discipline with only the best interest of your child in mind, asking yourself the following questions:

How will this discipline help my child?

What lesson will they learn?

What lesson am I trying to teach my child?

Disciplining your child cannot be about you; it must be about your child. I am thankful my Heavenly Father only disciplines His children with their best interests at heart.

Remember to be reasonable. Make the punishment fit the crime. For example, Alice Johnson was serving a life sentence for a nonviolent drug offense. Kalief Browder, 16 years old, spent three years in Rikers Island, even though he had not been convicted of a crime. Those are examples of over-punishment. Believe it or not, parents do the same with their children, sometimes punishing too harshly.

When I was a preschool director, I called a student's parents to tell them that their child had done something that needed to be addressed, but it was not a major problem. The issue was the typical behavior of a five-year-old learning self-control, but not behavior that should continue. Because of this, I wanted the parents to know so that they could talk with their child. The student's mom and dad came to my office, and after telling them the account of what happened, I could tell they were incredibly angry at their child. They said they were going to cancel his birthday party and take away a few other things. The look on my face caused them to ask me if I thought they were overreacting.

"Absolutely," I responded.

I told them that this was typical behavior, but I wanted them to know so they could talk to and teach their child. I'm not sure why they reacted so drastically. Maybe they were embarrassed. We've all been there.

Nevertheless, we should not overreact with discipline. Telling a child they can't play with their friends for one month might be a bit excessive. I knew of a mother that made her sons crawl on rice on their bare knees if they dirtied their pants at school.

Is that discipline or cruelty?

What four-year-old won't dirty their pants at the knees from time to time?

That same parent put her five-year-old child out of the car and made him run beside her car on a busy highway for being noisy on the way to school. Who is really out of line? The child or the mom?

Please review the following tips to ensure you are disciplining for the right reasons instead of disciplining in anger.

Tip #1: *Do not discipline in anger. Take an adult timeout if needed.*

It is perfectly okay to take a timeout. Give yourself time to think so you do not react in anger. Be reasonable. Stay balanced when it comes to discipline. Do not turn discipline into provocation. Do not provoke children to anger. We never want discipline to feel like hatred. State why you are punishing them, share as much wisdom about the situation, and then let your child know how much you love them. Do not spend large amounts of time disciplining. Discipline, then move on. Discipline is an important part of the growth in a child's life. Our responsibility is to teach our children, but remember that discipline must always be grounded in love.

Tip #2: *For discipline to be most effective, your words must be heard.*

Calm down so you can be heard. You are trying to nurture your child and give wisdom, not impart anger. If you are going to make taking care of your children a joy and not a job, commit to never disciplining in anger. It is entirely possible to correct a child without yelling and spanking.

But to spank or not to spank?

That is the question.

I thought long and hard about whether to include this section in the book but decided it was necessary because there are parents that spank. It's interesting how people feel differently about this topic, yet both sides are convinced they are right, and the other side is stupid for their approach. If you are wholeheartedly against spanking, please feel free to skip this part and move on to Chapter 10.

Let's start from the beginning with the practice of spanking from a Christian viewpoint. Spanking is a practice whose foundation came from the Old Testament of the Bible and was passed down from generation to generation. In the Bible, several scriptures discuss physical discipline and dealing with children, including the following from the Old Testament:

"The rod and reproof give wisdom: but a child left to himself bringeth his mother to shame."

(Proverbs 29:15)

"He that spareth his rod hateth his son: but he that loveth him chasteneth him often."
(Proverbs 13:24)

"Chasten thy son while there is hope, and let not thy soul spare for his crying."
(Proverbs 19:18)

"Foolishness is bound in the heart of a child, but the rod of correction shall drive it far from him."
(Proverbs 22:15)

"Withhold not correction from the child: for if thou beatest him with the rod, he shall not die. Thou shalt beat him with the rod, and shalt deliver his soul from hell (i.e., death)."
(Proverbs 23:13-14)

In the New Testament:

"For whom the Lord loveth he chasteneth, and scourgeth
every son whom he receiveth. If ye endure chastening, God
dealeth with you as with sons; for what son is he whom the
father chasteneth not?"

(Hebrews 12:6-7)

"Children obey your parents in the Lord, for this is right.
Honor thy father and mother. This is the first commandment
with promise. If you honor your father and mother, it shall be
well with you."

(Ephesians 6:1)

"And they brought unto him also infants, that he would touch
them: but when his disciples saw it, they rebuked them. But
Jesus called them unto him, and said, 'Suffer little children to
come unto me, and forbid them not: for of such is the kingdom
of God.'"

(Luke 18:15-16)

"At the same time came the disciples unto Jesus, saying,
'Who is the greatest in the kingdom of heaven?' And Jesus
called a little child unto him, and set him in the midst of them,

And said, 'Verily I say unto you, except ye be converted, and become as little children, ye shall not enter into the kingdom of heaven. Whosoever, therefore, shall humble himself as this little child, the same is greatest in the kingdom of heaven. And whoso shall receive one such little child in my name receiveth me. But whoso shall offend one of these little ones which believe in me, it were better for him that a millstone were hanged about his neck and that he were drowned in the depth of the sea.'"

(Matthew 18:1-6)

"And, ye fathers, provoke not your children to wrath: but bring them up in the nurture and admonition of the Lord."

(Ephesians 6:4)

The scriptures mentioned above in the Old and New Testaments speak about children. The focus seems slightly different in each Testament. In the Old Testament, it is very clear that the scriptures are talking about physical discipline. It goes so far as to say that if you discipline your child, you love them, and if you don't discipline your child, you hate them. In the New Testament, the scripture in Hebrews talks about the Lord disciplining His children. There seems to be more emphasis on not provoking children, nurturing them, and admonishing adults to be like children. There is even a warning for offending a child.

We know spanking has been a practice in our society passed down from generation to generation for a very long time. How have the past generations of spanked children fared? Many amazing people have been spanked, amazing human beings who have become wonderful in their craft – presidents, doctors, lawyers, teachers, moms, dads, and friends, and so forth. You also have terrible human beings who were spanked. Some people became evil, did terrible things, were terrible at their craft, and were terrible mothers, fathers, and friends. The dichotomy is staggering. So, there are people who faired well with spanking and others that did not.

In our society, spanking was an accepted punishment for children until new parenting ideas were on the horizon. I'm sure others had introduced such ideas, but this time it would stick with a doctor by the name of Dr. Spock.

Benjamin McLane Spock was an American pediatrician whose book *Baby and Child Care* is one of the best-selling books in history. The book's premise to mothers is that "you know more than you think you do" (Spock and Dorothea Warren Fox 2013). I read this on Dr. Spock's homepage and felt compelled to share:

You know more than you think you do. You want to be the best parent you can be, but it's not always clear what's best. There's so much information out there; it's hard to know what to listen to. Everyone has an opinion. What made sense a generation ago may not work anymore. Don't take too seriously what your friends and family tell you. Don't be awed by the experts. Trust your own common sense. Bringing up your child doesn't have to be complicated if you take it easy and rely on your instincts. The natural loving care that parents give their children is a hundred times more important than knowing how to make a diaper fit tightly or just when to start solid foods. Every time you pick your baby up and feed her, change her, smile at her, she's getting the feeling that she belongs to you and that you belong to her ("Dr. Benjamin Spock" 2015).

Elizabeth Gershoff, Ph.D., Associate Professor of Human Development and Family Sciences at the University of Texas at Austin, stated that spanking is a euphemism for hitting. "We convince ourselves that hitting children is okay" (Picard 2017). In other words, while many parents keep corporal punishment in their disciplinary toolbox, something feels wrong with it. The research explains why: Spanking has serious long-term effects, and we need to talk about it. "Spanking actually makes children worse behaved over the long term," Gershoff says. "They actually get harder to parent" (Picard 2017). Furthermore, Gershoff shares that the results of spanking are "fairly damning":

Spanking was associated with aggression, antisocial behavior, mental health problems, low self-esteem, negative parent-child relationships, impaired cognitive ability, externalizing behavior problems, internalizing behavior problems, and low moral internalization. A whopping 99% of the statistically significant data showed a link between spanking and a detrimental child outcome.

Again, it is important to mention this statistic: 78% of child abuse is done by a parent.

According to these experts, spanking is a detriment to your child. So, are people who were not spanked amazing, well-rounded people who are loving and do not suffer from mental illness, aggression, antisocial behavior, mental health problems, low self-esteem, negative parent-child relationships? If the answer to that question is yes, we might have our answer of whether to spank, but we don't have that answer. Yes, some non-spanked people are great, but unfortunately, some are not. Both sides have compelling arguments, and I am inclined to believe that the answer falls somewhere in the middle. We have become extreme both ways. Maybe the problem is not the method but the administrator of the method.

In 2013, I took a child development class, and we discussed this topic. One of the young ladies in class that didn't have children began to share how spanking causes children to be mentally ill. Maybe if she had said spanking could cause mental illness, I probably would have agreed. Mentally, I examined my family. At the time of this class lecture, I had already raised six children, who I had spanked, and my children did not have mental illness as a result. My mother raised eight children, whom she spanked. None of her children have mental illnesses. So, I thought that the student's statement was interesting. I wasn't offended, just baffled. There was something amiss with her statement. There are too many people in our society that were spanked that are not mentally ill. How did they escape this effect of spanking?

Part of the problem is this: Some parents spank for just about anything, any time the child is disobedient, or does something that the parent does not like.

How many parents spank because they want their friends and family to think they are tough disciplinarians?

How many parents spank because they feel the Bible gives them a pass?

How many parents spank just because this is what their parents did to them?

Too many!

On the other hand, how many parents feel that if they discipline their children, they do not love them?

How many parents allow their children to be disobedient to the point of it being dangerous?

How many parents allow their children to do whatever the child wants to do?

Too many!

Where is the balance? We must be careful not to become extreme in dealing with our children, such as spanking for everything nor allowing children to be raised without any instructions; constantly yelling nor being afraid to say no to a child because they will throw a tantrum; being restrictive with children that they can't do anything nor allowing children to do whatever they want to do. Where is the balance?

How many parents teach their children the importance and benefits of being obedient instead of spanking to enforce obedience?

Ephesians 6:1-3 states:

Children, obey your parents in the Lord: for this is right. Honour thy father and mother; which is the first commandment with promise; That it may be well with thee, and thou mayest live long on the earth.

Ephesians 6:1-3 speaks directly to children. How does a child know this scripture is speaking to them unless a parent teaches it? Teach Ephesians 6:1-3 to your children. It was a scripture I started teaching my children early. I even put this scripture to a tune, and we would sing it. Teach them the benefits of obedience and the consequences of disobedience.

When the Old Testament tells us that the rod and reproof bring wisdom, I believe that is the answer to the question about spanking; however, parents want to spank but forget about reproof. Teaching children requires time, but many do not take the time to teach, so they spank; however, spanking is not effective by itself. Children go to school to learn, but the lessons they need to be taught to be successful, decent humans must be taught in the home by parents.

Spanking is useful, but like anything else, it loses its power when it is abused. Spanking without reproof is abuse. We have abused spanking for far too long in our society, and our children suffer because of it. If you add reproof to discipline, you will find that you will not need to spank as much or maybe not at all, depending on your child.

In Matthew 18:3, the Lord encourages adults to become like little children: "And he said, 'Truly I tell you, unless you change and become like little children, you will never enter the kingdom of heaven.'"

Adults often encourage children to become like us, but the Lord says we should become like them in some things. If you apologize to your children, they are quick to forgive, unlike adults that hold on to grudges, sometimes for a lifetime. Children do not create differences between people unless they are taught. They will love anyone unless they are taught differently. On the other hand, adults will hate someone because they don't agree politically or spiritually. We are rude in the workplace, and we backbite and treat people terribly, yet we are in charge of helping our little people become good humans.

Ephesians 6:4 states, "Father, provoke not your child to anger, lest they be discouraged." I'm sure the saying is true for mothers as well. When we yell and discipline in anger, we provoke our children to anger and discourage them. In Ephesians 6:4, Jesus is discouraging maltreatment of children, and I love it.

In Matthew 19:13-15, we see Jesus' heart for the little children:

Then were there brought unto him (Jesus) little children, that he should put his hands on them, and pray: and the disciples rebuked them. But Jesus said, Suffer little children, and forbid them not, to come unto me: for of such is the kingdom of heaven. And he laid his hands on them and departed thence (Matthew 19:13-15).

Jesus, the God of the world, has the time to lay hands on children and tell the adults not to hinder the little children from coming to Him. When you take the time to lay your hands on your child and pray for them, you connect differently and will never want to hurt or abuse them with your words or hands.

My problem with dismissing spanking is that it is a biblical principle. While man is intelligent, they will never know more than God. And just because something is a biblical principle does not mean it cannot be abused. I don't believe spanking is immoral, but man is immoral. Therefore, man's abuse of spanking becomes immoral. Food is not immoral, but man's abuse of food makes it so. That is why we have TV shows like *My 600-lb Life*. Shopping is not immoral, but man makes it so, and that's why we have TV shows like *Hoarders*. Sex is not immoral, but man makes it so, which is why there is rape, incest, and sex trafficking. The human element makes them sinful. Again, maybe the problem is not the method of spanking but the administrator. Maybe the problem with spanking is the adult.

If you struggle with anger and a lack of self-control, you should not spank. Parents must grow and become better, and until parents can control their anger, they should use other methods of discipline. When adults spank in anger, it is too easy to cross the line into abuse. When parents can't control their anger yet spank their children, this is a major problem. The Bible says that rod and reproof bring wisdom, so you can't just spank and never have these great conversations of reproof if you want your child to be wise (Proverbs 29:15). Discipline is not about you but helping the child be an asset to the people they encounter.

Spanking is a personal choice until it becomes a legal issue. Currently, in most states and countries, spanking is legal. My advice, however, is to spank less and reprove more.

This means that more time must be spent with your child, teaching, instructing, and giving wisdom. In a time when child abuse, child neglect, child trafficking, and child slavery are on the upswing, we need to be very careful to love and protect our precious little ones. Remember, if you are an adult who does not control your emotions, you should not spank.

Our society is starting to lump spanking and abuse in the same category, and I don't think that is fair. In general, spanking and abuse are not the same. Unfortunately, spanking is abuse in far too many situations because adults are too comfortable crossing this line. I wrestled with this topic but finally concluded that God is right and everyone else is wrong. Spanking is not bad in and of itself; it's bad when adults take it to a bad place with anger. I must side with the Word of God in that spanking is a biblical principle but needs to be handled with as much care and love of the Savior that died on the cross for you and me.

Looking back, I disciplined my children according to my knowledge. I genuinely tried to make the choices about discipline that would help my children be better, wiser, and smarter. I wanted to help them be the best they could be. If I were raising my children all over again, there would be situations in which I would still spank. I would spend as much time teaching and giving my children wisdom that they could live on for years to come.

Chapter 9

At a Glance

Assess yourself truthfully. Do you fall into anger easily? Do you lose control easily? If the answer is yes, you should not spank. Gain control of your life to help your child gain control of their life.

Do not spank because your child has made you mad or has gotten on your last nerve. Disciplining is not about you. You must change to help your child.

Are you disciplining your children for the right reasons? If not, what can you change?

The goal is to focus on never disciplining your child in anger. Take a timeout and walk away, but do not act in anger. The results can be life-altering.

Chapter 10

Parent Your Children

"In one school year, a child spends 77,800 hours at home and 900 hours at school. Which teacher should be the most accountable?"

Jim Trelease

In the previous chapters, several topics were shared: parenting with joy, spending time with your children, not expecting what you have not taught, and taking off the blinders. Also discussed were yelling less, the importance of silence, rest, and self-care, being a safe place, never disciplining children in anger, and watching what we say to and about our children. So, this chapter is a healthy summary of parenting.

I often see parents allow the little people in their homes to run things instead of parenting the same little people that came into this world with no knowledge. They start not knowing how to walk, talk, read, and comprehend, yet they are practically in charge at three years old. These are the same little people who eat boogers, play with spit, stick their fingers in electrical sockets, and lick frozen metal poles. Yet, they determine what the family will eat for dinner, what everyone will watch on TV, and when everyone will go to bed. If they want to stay up until midnight, then the parents stay up until midnight. You, the parent, understand that staying up late is not great for productivity, not to mention not good for your body. Children will eat candy and snacks all day because they do not know what is good for them.

So, why do children do those things?

Because they don't know any better, but you do.

Children should have choices, but children don't have enough knowledge about everything to make informed decisions.

These little people need to be parented. Be careful with the decisions you leave in the hands of children. You can't imagine the weight of responsibility that children take on when allowed to make adult decisions. Children should be allowed to be children, not carrying the weight of their family on their shoulders. From time to time, I've seen children riding in a car without a seat belt. Who made this decision?

Because the child did not want to get in a car seat, you allowed them to stand in a moving car? This is something a child should not choose. Riding in a car seat and being strapped in is the law. Have you ever seen a parent that allowed their child to run things? It's difficult to watch. I saw a parent crying to her child, asking why he doesn't listen to Mommy. He was three. Children should not train parents; parents should train children.

Again, it is reasonable for children to have choices. Maybe they choose where the family eats on a certain day. Maybe they choose which movie the family will watch on certain nights or what clothes they will wear for certain occasions. Your child may want to wear shorts and a T-shirt on a day when it is freezing outside. You know that is not appropriate or safe. There are some things children should be allowed to choose and things they should not choose.

There are some things that their little minds don't understand. They may want to drive a car at five, but they can't make that decision any more than they can decide to vote at age ten. The Lord wants parents to parent their children with as much love and care as possible. He wants us to give them instruction but also lead by example. Children will do what they see, even when their parents are not aware that their children saw. If you don't want your child to use bad language, do not use it in front of them. A friend once said to me, "What you do in moderation, your children will do in excess."

Recently, I saw a post on my daughter's Facebook page about an interaction she had with her oldest child, my granddaughter:

Daughter rolls eyes

Mom: We never taught you how to do that.

Daughter: Yes, you did.

Mom: How or when?

Daughter: Because of all the times you roll your eyes at Daddy.

The lesson was not with words but actions. Whatever it is, just know your children see you and will do what you do.

Let your no be no and your yes be yes. Do not say no to your child if you do not mean it. If you let your child do something, why say no just to let them do it anyway. This can be confusing for your child.

Do not make false threats like, "If you don't stop, I will send you to your room," yet when the child does not stop, the parents do not send the child to their room. You just taught your child not to believe what you say and that you can be disrespected.

Also, do not make hyperbolic statements like, "I'm going to knock your head off" or "I'm going to ground you forever." Both are unfeasible and absurd.

Parents often think a child's teacher will teach them all the important things they will need in this life. You, the parent, are responsible for teaching your child. You will teach them everything, whereas your child's teacher will not begin to scratch the surface. The teacher's classroom ratio is often 1:20 or 1:30, depending on the size of the class. Your ratio is 1:1, 1:2, or 1:6, depending on the number of children you have. Who do you think should have more impact, parents or teachers? Parents, let's accept responsibility for the training of our children. Train in joy through these tips:

Tip #1: *Love is the number one component in teaching children, but it is not the only thing.*

Love will help you get through. Love is stronger than death. Love makes us all better. Do everything for and with your child in love.

Tip #2: *Along with love, you will need wisdom.*

In the multitude of counsel, there is safety (Proverbs 11:14). If you don't know, pray, talk to friends, family, counselors, read books, seek help, and follow your gut.

Be confident.

Make decisions.

Parent!

Settle in, strap on your boots, and get ready to go.

Parenting is not a sprint; this is a marathon filled with victories and defeats, good times, tough times, ups and downs.

You are not alone in the race. Many people have run this race, and you can do it, too. Don't give up, and don't give in. Stay strong! Repeat this note to self: I know better than my child about most things.

In writing this book, I had many conversations with my children to get their perspectives. It was a bit challenging to write because I had to confront myself as a parent. As mentioned before, there were some things I got right, mistakes I made, lessons I learned, and notes to self I made along the way. There are things I would do differently and some things I would keep the same. I would have narrowed my focus to be more protective and nurturing, soaking up every moment more. I would have listened more and been more present. I would have laughed and hugged more because, when looking back, that's what matters. The thing is, there is no going back. We don't get to undo our past. We only have today. I hope something was shared on these pages to help you get the most out of your today and every day with your children.

Parenting is still my greatest joy. I am now a mother of six adult children and seven grandchildren with one on the way, and my joy is no less than the first day I laid eyes on my first sweet baby girl. My heart hopes that anyone who has read these pages finds the same joy in parenting. I wish you restful nights, prosperous days, and amazing relationships with your children to last a lifetime.

Every parent leaves an inheritance to their children. Some do it purposefully, and others do it by accident, but we all leave an inheritance. Our hope as parents is to leave money, cars, houses, and land to our children, but we must leave more. For parents without great financial means to leave their children, that does not mean they cannot leave them an inheritance.

Lately, I have gone to two estate sales. One of the people I knew was well respected in her community, the other a stranger, but my experience was the same at both sales. I felt incredibly sad at the sale and sadder after I left. At these sales, there were valuable items that the parents had collected throughout their lifetime – beautiful furniture, jewelry, paintings, art pieces, dishes, amazing books, lawn equipment, tools, cars, houses – items that a parent works so hard for that the children have no desire to keep. This type of inheritance is awesome, even if the children sell it and get the money. Unfortunately, unless that money is invested, that inheritance will only last for a short time.

I want to encourage you to leave an inheritance that can never be taken away – an inheritance of love:

An inheritance for your child to know they were loved.

An inheritance of wise words that your children can hear ringing in their ears and pass on to their children.

An inheritance of faith. Let your children see you walking in faith toward God and trusting Him, especially during the tough times of life.

An inheritance of joy that your children see that it is possible to maintain joy; although weeping may come for a night season, joy always comes in the morning season (Psalm 30:5).

Shannon L. Alder said, "It's not what you leave to your children that matters, but what you leave in them." So, leave an inheritance that money can't buy. Leave an inheritance that the world can't take from your children. Leave something for their spirits, for their inner man. Leave them whole, not torn apart from your actions or shredded by your words, but whole in body, spirit, and soul.

When I was about ten years old, I challenged my mother to a race. I knew there was no way my mom could beat me. She was old, or at least that's what I thought. She was actually just shy of 40. I was so surprised when Mom won. In fact, she breezed by me in that race. Fast forward 20-

something years later, My mom is in her 60s and in the backyard with my children, her grandchildren. I'm not sure how the challenge went down, but my mom raced my children, and guess what? She beat them! Maybe not destroyed them, but she won nonetheless. Fast forward 20-something years later, mom is now in her 80s. There is a video of my mother running with her great-granddaughter in a field. When I tell you that is the most beautiful thing I have seen. That is inheritance.

Me, as a child, watching my mother make sure all the older people in my community had a Christmas gift, even though she was a single parent of eight… that's inheritance.

Me, as a child, watching my mother handle situations with such grace, never being angry when others were angry with her… that's inheritance.

Me, as a child, watching my mother in worship. My friends and I would watch to see whose mom would "catch the spirit" first. When they worshiped, she would lose herself and be in her own world. I love watching her worship to this day… that's inheritance.

Me, having other strong women to invest in my life: my Aunt Lula, who poured into my life with prayers and spiritual encouragement; my Aunt Medora, taking the time to know the birthdays of her nieces and nephews, great-nieces, and nephews so that she could send a gift every year; my Aunt Barbara shopping throughout the year and having clothes on hand, especially to give to my young children and other children; my sisters Cookie, Say, Bonnie, and Shawn, my friends from day one who have always loved and supported me; my cousins, Lhonita and Whonita, that loved me and made me feel special... this is my inheritance!

Inheritance is leaving your children something that will outlive them, something that has value and can be passed on from generation to generation, such as how we treat people, serve people, and show love for one another and our fellow man. Someone once said the best inheritance a parent can give their children is their time each day. Now that's inheritance!

Looking back, I got so much information on how to be a parent from different sources: my mom, books, friends, and others I observed in the role of parenting. I took tips from others and would try them with my children. If they worked, great! If not, I would try something different. I thought if I did my best as a mom and kept my children's best interests in the forefront, things would turn out okay. I tried to treat my children in a way that I would have no regrets about later in life. I tried my best not to over stress what I could not control. I knew more than anything that love had to be the driving force of anything I did with my children. So, the advice that Miss Susie gave me became the guiding light that helped influence the way I parented, and it's been the best ~~job~~ joy I've ever had.

Chapter 10

At a Glance

You are the parent.

You set the tone.

You have the responsibility to leave your child whole.

The goal of this book is to encourage you to find joy in parenting, to help you create a safe space for your children in this crazy world, and to encourage you toward an amazing relationship with your children. This book was written to help parents reject the negative things the world tells them about raising children. It encourages parents to soak up every moment with their children and invest heavily in their relationship.

It was written to encourage parents to never cross the line between discipline and abuse so that children are not damaged by anger because they become damaged adults.

It was written to encourage parents to look down the road and think about the type of relationship they want with their children when they are adults and encourages each parent to put in the work for that relationship now. These words are to encourage you to spend time talking to your children when they are young so they will be comfortable talking to you when they are adults.

This book was written to remind you that a tree cannot grow outside of its proper environment. Trees grow in different environments, but it must be the proper environment. Create the best environment so that your child grows up to be a happy, whole, healthy adult.

Again, this book was written to remind you that you can choose to parent with joy, and the choice is up to you. You can do it! You can make taking care of your children a joy and not a job. I pray you have been blessed as you have read the pages of this book. I am sending blessings above and beyond to your family.

Extra Joy

"If you bungle raising your children, I don't think whatever else you do matters very much."

Jackie Kennedy

While spending your time with your children, remain open to learning lessons from them, such as:

- *How to forgive quickly.* Children can fight one moment and be the best of friends in the next.
- *How to be honest.* Children have not learned to teach their tongues to lie. They usually speak the truth.
- *Not holding grudges.*
- *Not to discriminate, judge, or treat people differently based on race, ethnicity, and religion.* Unless taught otherwise, children love everyone.

Also, please remember:

We send mixed messages to our children. If you are mad at your children for fighting but always talk about beating up somebody, that's confusing for them.

Let your care for your child start in the womb by speaking kind words, singing, and sharing kind thoughts. Be careful with the way you treat children:

But whoso shall offend one of these little ones which believe in me, it were better for him that a millstone were hanged about his neck, and that he were drowned in the depth of the sea (Matthew 18:6).

Practice staying in hugs. I once had someone tell me to hold on to hugs with my children until they let go. Don't rush through those moments. I still practice this today, even though they are adults.

Teach your children to deal with finances and start early. This is one thing that most schools do not teach enough about, but you can as a parent.

Find that sweet balance between love and discipline, fun and order, and peace with a bit of chaos. I am praying for you, Mom and Dad, and wishing you the greatest joy of all. Make taking care of your children a joy and not a job.

Sources

American SPCC. 2014. "Child Abuse Statistics - American
   SPCC." American SPCC. 2014. https://americanspcc.org/
   child-abuse-statistics/.

Clear, James. 2017. *Atomic Habits.* Penguin Publishing
   Group.

Dawson, Ben. 2020. "The State of America's Children 2020."
   Children's Defense Fund. 2020. https://
   www.childrensdefense.org/the-state-of-americas-
   children-2020/.

"Dictionary by Merriam-Webster: America's Most-Trusted
   Online Dictionary." n.d. Www.merriam-Webster.com.
   https://www.merriamwebster.com

Don Miguel Ruiz. 2008. *The Four Agreements.* Hay House
   Inc.

Gervis, Zoya. 2018. "Parents Spend an Insane Amount of
   Their Lives Worrying about Their Kids." New York
   Post. September 10, 2018. https://nypost.com/
   2018/09/10/parents-spend-an-insane-amount-of-their-
   lives-worrying-about-their-kids/.

"Homepage - Dr. Benjamin Spock." 2015. Dr. Benjamin
Spock. 2015. https://drspock.com.

Jenn, Sturiale. n.d. "Stop Yelling at Your Kids." WebMD.
Accessed September 8, 2021. https://www.webmd.com/
parenting/features/stop-yelling-at-your-kids.

"Joy Noun - Definition, Pictures, Pronunciation and Usage
Notes | Oxford Advanced Learner's Dictionary at
OxfordLearnersDictionaries.com." 2021.
www.oxfordlearnersdictionaries.com. 2021. https://
www.oxfordlearnersdictionaries.com/definition/
english/joy.

National Children's Alliance. 2019. "National Child Abuse
Statistics from NCA." National Children's Alliance. 2019.
www.nationalchildrensalliance.org/media-room/national-
statistics-on-child-abuse/.

Picard, Caroline. 2017. "How Bad Is Spanking, Really?"
Good Housekeeping. November 8, 2017.
www.goodhousekeeping.com/life/parenting/a46709/
effects-of-spanking/.

Shelly Vaziri Flais, and American Academy Of Pediatrics. 2018. *Caring for Your School-Age Child: Ages 5 to 12.* New York: Bantam Books.

Spock, Benjamin, and Dorothea Warren Fox. 2013. *The Common Sense Book of Baby and Child Care.* Bronx, NY: Ishi Press International.

"Stop Comparing Your Child with Others - Being the Parent." 2016. BeingTheParent.com. April 15, 2016. www.beingtheparent.com/stop-comparing-your-child/.

"Why Do Kids Bully?" 2005. Www.stompoutbullying.org. 2005. www.stompoutbullying.org/why-kids-bully.

"Unwrapping the Link between Childhood Trauma and Health." 2021. EndCAN. January 20, 2021. https://endcan.org/2021/01/20/unwrapping-the-link-between-childhood-trauma-and-health/.

"Young Women's Christian Association." 2021. YWCA USA. 2021. www.ywca.org.

Zahed, Dr. Hyder. 2014. "The Power of Spoken Words." The Huffington Post. December 15, 2014. https://www.huffpost.com/entry/the-power-of-spoken-words_b_6324786#:~:text=%22Words%20are%20singularly%20the%20most.

Printed in Poland
by Amazon Fulfillment
Poland Sp. z o.o., Wrocław